W9-CNH-550

SHURLEY ENGLISH

HOMESCHOOL MADE EASY

LEVEL 1

Student Book

By
Brenda Shurley

Shurley Instructional Materials, Inc., Cabot, Arkansas

01-21
Shurley English Homeschooling
Level 1 Student Workbook
ISBN 978-1-58561-049-5

Copyright © 2002 by Shurley Instructional Materials, Inc.
No part of this book may be reproduced or transmitted in any form or by any means, electronic or mechanical, including photocopying, recording, or by any information storage or retrieval system, without written permission from the Publisher.

Printed in the United States of America by Bradford & Bigelow, Newburyport, MA.

For additional information or to place an order, write to: Shurley Instructional Materials, Inc.
366 SIM Drive
Cabot, AR 72023

1 2 3 4 5 6 7 8 9 10 11 12 13 21 19 17 16 15 14 13 11 09 07 05 03 02

JINGLE

SECTION

Jingle Section

Jingle 1: Noun Jingle

This little noun
Floating around
Names a person, place, or thing.
With a knick knack, paddy wack,
These are English rules.
Isn't language fun and cool?

Jingle 2: Verb Jingle

A verb shows action,
There's no doubt!
It tells what the
subject does,
Like sing and shout.

Action verbs are fun to do.
Now, it's time to name a few.
So, clap your hands
And join our rhyme;
Say those verbs
In record time!

Wiggle, jiggle, turn around;
Raise your arms
And stomp the ground.
Shake your finger
And wink your eye;
Wave those action verbs
good-bye.

Jingle 3: Sentence Jingle

A sentence, sentence, sentence
Is complete, complete, complete
When 5 simple rules
It meets, meets, meets.

It has a subject, subject, subject
And a verb, verb, verb.
It makes sense, sense, sense
With every word, word, word.

Add a capital letter, letter
And an end mark, mark.
Now, we're finished, and aren't we smart!
Now, our sentence has all its parts!

REMEMBER
Subject, Verb, Com-plete sense,
Capital letter, and an end mark, too.
That's what a sentence is all about!

© SHURLEY INSTRUCTIONAL MATERIALS, INC.

Jingle Section

Jingle 4: Adverb Jingle

An adverb modifies a verb.
An adverb asks *How? When? Where?*
To find an adverb: **Go, Ask, Get**.
Where do I **go**? To a verb.
What do I **ask**? How? When? Where?
What do I **get**? An ADVERB! (Clap) (Clap) That's what!

Jingle 5: Adjective Jingle

An adjective modifies a noun.
An adjective asks *What kind? Which one? How many?*
To find an adjective: **Go, Ask, Get**.
Where do I **go**? To a noun.
What do I **ask**? What kind? Which one? How many?
What do I **get**? An ADJECTIVE! (Clap) (Clap) That's what!

Jingle 6: Article Adjective Jingle

We are the article adjectives,
Teeny, tiny adjectives:
A, AN, THE - A, AN, THE.

We are called article adjectives and noun markers;
We are memorized and used every day.
So, if you spot us, you can mark us
With the label A.

We are the article adjectives,
Teeny, tiny adjectives:
A, AN, THE - A, AN, THE.

© SHURLEY INSTRUCTIONAL MATERIALS, INC.

Jingle Section

Jingle 7: Preposition Jingle

A PREP PREP PREPOSITION
Is a special group of words
That connects a
NOUN, NOUN, NOUN
Or a PRO, PRO, PRONOUN
To the rest of the sentence.

Jingle 8: Object of the Prep Jingle

Dum De Dum Dum!
An O-P is a N-O-U-N or a P-R-O
After the P-R-E-P
In a S-E-N-T-E-N-C-E.
Dum De Dum Dum - DONE!

© SHURLEY INSTRUCTIONAL MATERIALS, INC.

VOCABULARY

SECTION

VOCABULARY TIME – LEVEL 1

Chapter 6, Vocabulary Words #1	Chapter 6, Vocabulary Words #2
cats, boys, bears, sat, ran	girls, dogs, played

Chapter 6, Vocabulary Words #3	Chapter 6, Vocabulary Words #4
walked, airplanes, flew	ducks, barked, kittens

Chapter 7, Vocabulary Words #1	Chapter 7, Vocabulary Words #2
quietly, today, fast	quickly, loudly, slowly

Chapter 7, Vocabulary Words #3	Chapter 7, Vocabulary Words #4
swiftly, yesterday, low	away, jumped, puppies

Chapter 8, Vocabulary Words #1	Chapter 8, Vocabulary Words #2
two, black, big, brown	three, laughed, squirmy

Chapter 8, Vocabulary Words #3	Chapter 8, Vocabulary Words #4
several, little, happily, four	yellow, waddled, children

Chapter 9, Vocabulary Words #1	Chapter 9, Vocabulary Words #2
yawned, horse, raced	excited, shouted, tired

Chapter 9, Vocabulary Words #3	Chapter 9, Vocabulary Words #4
large, ships, sailed, rapidly	busy, beavers, worked

Chapter 10, Vocabulary Words #1	Chapter 10, Vocabulary Words #2
stopped, suddenly, clowns	five, home, cute, baby

Chapter 10, Vocabulary Words #3	Chapter 10, Vocabulary Words #4
unhappy, cried, happy, six	hungry, birds, monkeys

Chapter 11, Vocabulary Words #1	Chapter 11, Vocabulary Words #2
silly, around, beautiful, car	weary, brothers, ants, crawled, noisily

Chapter 11, Vocabulary Words #3	Chapter 11, Vocabulary Words #4
students, hard, lazy, green, frog	funny, shy, fox, thin

© SHURLEY INSTRUCTIONAL MATERIALS, INC.

Vocabulary – Level 1 (continued)

Chapter 12, Vocabulary Words #1	Chapter 12, Vocabulary Words #2
tiger, seven, balloon, floated	giant, slept, soundly, hopped

Chapter 12, Vocabulary Words #3	Chapter 12, Vocabulary Words #4
jets, landed, frightened, ate	red, flowers, grew, pretty

Chapter 13, Vocabulary Words #1	Chapter 13, Vocabulary Words #2
house, smoothly, runway, shade, (to, on, in)	bee, softly, poor, fell, mud, (by)

Chapter 13, Vocabulary Words #3	Chapter 13, Vocabulary Words #4
huge, snake, road, tiny, (across, at)	friends, movies, dime, door

Chapter 14, Vocabulary Words #1	Chapter 14, Vocabulary Words #2
jelly, jar, floor, lake	music, store, camped, mountains

Chapter 14, Vocabulary Words #3	Chapter 14, Vocabulary Words #4
rabbit, rain, waited, bus	window, waved, passengers, looked, bananas

Chapter 15, Vocabulary Words #1	Chapter 15, Vocabulary Words #2
grasshopper, garden, deer, swans	family, beach, crib, eight, small

Chapter 15, Vocabulary Words #3	Chapter 15, Vocabulary Words #4
church, old, gray, white, (down)	shivering, whimpered, ocean, crashed, rocks

Chapter 16, Vocabulary Words #1	Chapter 16, Vocabulary Words #2
kites, high, sky	nine, silently, rolled

Chapter 16, Vocabulary Words #3	Chapter 16, Vocabulary Words #4
pony, trotted, pink, pig	bell, rang, valley, sailor, map

Chapter 17, Vocabulary Words #1	Chapter 17, Vocabulary Words #2
rode, train, went, zoo	sun, city, opened, early, pond

Chapter 17, Vocabulary Words #3	Chapter 17, Vocabulary Words #4
library, book, carefully, ice	volcano, erupted, ten, swam

Chapter 18, Vocabulary Words #1	Chapter 18, Vocabulary Words #2
Tim, street, otters, water, salty, popcorn	clever, field, new, sleds, hill

Chapter 18, Vocabulary Words #3	Chapter 18, Vocabulary Words #4
snow, shines, brightly, gate	barn, mouse, James

© SHURLEY INSTRUCTIONAL MATERIALS, INC.

Vocabulary – Level 1 (continued)

Chapter 19, Vocabulary Words #1	Chapter 19, Vocabulary Words #2
log, wagon, scampered	Anna, fog, tall, Sam

Chapter 19, Vocabulary Words #3	Chapter 19, Vocabulary Words #4
gathered, roses, circus, pranced, proudly	kind, nurse, patient

Chapter 20, Vocabulary Words #1	Chapter 20, Vocabulary Words #2
excitedly, boat, fireflies, glowed, dark	animals, tree, mall

Chapter 20, Vocabulary Words #3	Chapter 20, Vocabulary Words #4
neighborhood, airport, strong, fished, stream	purple, summer, blue, blew

Chapter 21, Vocabulary Words #1	Chapter 21, Vocabulary Words #2
orange, socks	fireman, climbed, roof, butterfly, Dan

Chapter 21, Vocabulary Words #3	Chapter 21, Vocabulary Words #4
candles, burned, lost	Sarah, dressed, warmly, winter

Chapter 22, Vocabulary Words #1	Chapter 22, Vocabulary Words #2
ground, melted, goats, stood, porch	birthday, cake, pool

Chapter 22, Vocabulary Words #3	Chapter 22, Vocabulary Words #4
best, coins, path	hall, Mom, shopped, park

Chapter 23, Vocabulary Words #1	Chapter 23, Vocabulary Words #2
donkeys, geese	sand, truck, turned, pumpkins

Chapter 23, Vocabulary Words #3	Chapter 23, Vocabulary Words #4
young, smiled, spider	eggs, hatched, cheerfully, school

Chapter 24, Vocabulary Words #1	Chapter 24, Vocabulary Words #2
Grandmother, mailbox, together	bloomed, trail, camel, desert

Chapter 24, Vocabulary Words #3	Chapter 24, Vocabulary Words #4
eagle, gracefully, bouncy, grandchildren	raccoons, soldiers, marched, parade

Chapter 25, Vocabulary Words #1	Chapter 25, Vocabulary Words #2
stray, teacher, kindly	sisters, smoke, drifted, stared, hungrily, honey

Chapter 25, Vocabulary Words #3	Chapter 25, Vocabulary Words #4
bubbles, distant, twinkled, thick	angry, buzzed, overhead, beetle

© SHURLEY INSTRUCTIONAL MATERIALS, INC.

SYNONYM AND ANTONYM

SECTION

SYNONYM AND ANTONYM TIME – LEVEL 1

Chapter 7: Underline the **syn** if the words are synonyms. Underline the **ant** if the words are antonyms.

1. in, out	syn ant	2. right, wrong	syn ant	3. quit, stop	syn ant

Chapter 8: Underline the **syn** if the words are synonyms. Underline the **ant** if the words are antonyms.

1. over, under	syn ant	2. warm, cold	syn ant	3. stone, rock	syn ant

Chapter 9: Underline the **syn** if the words are synonyms. Underline the **ant** if the words are antonyms.

1. up, down	syn ant	2. push, pull	syn ant	3. start, begin	syn ant

Chapter 10: Underline the **syn** if the words are synonyms. Underline the **ant** if the words are antonyms.

1. giant, huge	syn ant	2. front, back	syn ant	3. rough, smooth	syn ant

Chapter 11: Underline the **syn** if the words are synonyms. Underline the **ant** if the words are antonyms.

1. form, shape	syn ant	2. inside, outside	syn ant	3. end, finish	syn ant

Chapter 12: Underline the **syn** if the words are synonyms. Underline the **ant** if the words are antonyms.

1. high, low	syn ant	2. open, close	syn ant	3. tiny, small	syn ant

Chapter 13: Underline the **syn** if the words are synonyms. Underline the **ant** if the words are antonyms.

1. far, near	syn ant	2. rush, hurry	syn ant	3. part, piece	syn ant

Chapter 14: Underline the **syn** if the words are synonyms. Underline the **ant** if the words are antonyms.

1. above, below	syn ant	2. old, new	syn ant	3. lean, thin	syn ant

Chapter 15: Underline the **syn** if the words are synonyms. Underline the **ant** if the words are antonyms.

1. left, right	syn ant	2. poor, rich	syn ant	3. puzzle, riddle	syn ant

© SHURLEY INSTRUCTIONAL MATERIALS, INC.

Synonym and Antonym – Level 1 (continued)

Chapter 16: Underline the **syn** if the words are synonyms. Underline the **ant** if the words are antonyms.

1. on, off	syn ant	2. tall, short	syn ant	3. kind, good	syn ant

Chapter 17: Underline the **syn** if the words are synonyms. Underline the **ant** if the words are antonyms.

1. top, bottom	syn ant	2. hard, firm	syn ant	3. evil, bad	syn ant

Chapter 18: Underline the **syn** if the words are synonyms. Underline the **ant** if the words are antonyms.

1. before, after	syn ant	2. lost, found	syn ant	3. sick, ill	syn ant

Chapter 19: Underline the **syn** if the words are synonyms. Underline the **ant** if the words are antonyms.

1. front, back	syn ant	2. early, late	syn ant	3. simple, easy	syn ant

Chapter 20: Underline the **syn** if the words are synonyms. Underline the **ant** if the words are antonyms.

1. first, last	syn ant	2. slow, quick	syn ant	3. raise, lift	syn ant

Chapter 21: Underline the **syn** if the words are synonyms. Underline the **ant** if the words are antonyms.

1. sweet, sour	syn ant	2. below, beneath	syn ant	3. aid, help	syn ant

Chapter 22: Underline the **syn** if the words are synonyms. Underline the **ant** if the words are antonyms.

1. night, day	syn ant	2. shout, whisper	syn ant	3. bashful, shy	syn ant

Chapter 23: Underline the **syn** if the words are synonyms. Underline the **ant** if the words are antonyms.

1. sell, buy	syn ant	2. ask, tell	syn ant	3. calm, quiet	syn ant

Chapter 24: Underline the **syn** if the words are synonyms. Underline the **ant** if the words are antonyms.

1. wild, tame	syn ant	2. add, subtract	syn ant	3. push, shove	syn ant

Chapter 25: Underline the **syn** if the words are synonyms. Underline the **ant** if the words are antonyms.

1. bright, dim	syn ant	2. round, square	syn ant	3. pull, tug	syn ant

© SHURLEY INSTRUCTIONAL MATERIALS, INC.

Notes

© SHURLEY INSTRUCTIONAL MATERIALS, INC.

REFERENCE

SECTION

Reference 1: Three Rules of a SENTENCE

1. The WORDS tell who or what the SENTENCE is about.
2. The WORDS tell what something does.
3. The WORDS should make complete sense.

Reference 2: What is Journal Writing?

Journal Writing is a written record of your personal thoughts and feelings about things or people that are important to you. You can record your dreams, memories, feelings, and experiences. You can ask questions and answer some of them. It is fun to go back later and read what you have written because it shows how you have changed in different areas of your life. Writing in a journal is an easy and enjoyable way to practice your writing skills without worrying about a writing grade.

What do I write about?

Journals are personal, but sometimes it helps to have ideas to get you started. Remember, in a journal, you do not have to stick to one topic. Write about someone or something you like. Write about what you did last weekend or on vacation. Write about what you hope to do this week or on your next vacation. Write about home, school, friends, hobbies, special talents (yours or someone else's), or the hopes and fears you have about things now and in the future. If something bothers you, record it in your journal. If something interests you, record it. After all, it is your journal!

How do I get started writing in my personal journal?

You need to put the day's date on the title line of your paper: **Month, Day, Year.** Skip the next line and begin your entry. You might write one or two sentences, a paragraph, a whole page, or several pages. Except for the journal date, no particular organizational style is required for journal writing. You decide how best to organize and express your thoughts. Feel free to include pictures or lists if they will help you remember your thoughts about different things. You will also need a spiral notebook, a pen, a quiet place, and at least 5-10 minutes of uninterrupted writing time.

Note: Any drawings you might include do not have to be masterpieces — stick figures will do nicely.

Reference 3: Synonyms and Antonyms

Definitions: Synonyms are words that have similar, or almost the same, meanings.
Antonyms are words that have opposite, or different, meanings.

Directions: Identify each pair of words as synonyms or antonyms by drawing a line under the ***syn*** or ***ant***.

1. small, tiny | **syn** ant |
2. up, down | syn **ant** |
3. happy, cheerful | **syn** ant |

© SHURLEY INSTRUCTIONAL MATERIALS, INC.

Reference 4: Definitions for Complete Subject, Complete Predicate
1. The **complete subject** is the subject and all the words that describe the subject. 2. The **complete predicate** is the verb and all the words that describe the verb. **Sample Sentence**: The little brown pony galloped swiftly yesterday.

Reference 5: Two Kinds of Sentences	
1. A **statement** is a sentence that tells something. A statement starts with a capital letter and ends with a period. Example: **T**he big bear walked away**.**	2. A **question** is a sentence that asks something. A question starts with a capital letter and ends with a question mark. Example: **D**o the boys work here**?**

Reference 6: Parts-of-Speech Word Bank			
On notebook paper, write a sentence using the words in the Word Bank. Put the words you select in the same order as the Sentence Labels listed below. Write the correct label above each word in your sentence.			
Nouns	**Verbs**	**Adjectives**	**Adverbs**
puppies kittens duck	barked, quacked, yawned, climbed, played, waddled, ran	a, an, the, two, black, yellow, brown, excited, sleepy, hungry, unhappy, cute, little	loudly, excitedly, fast, happily, rapidly, noisily, quietly, today
Sentence Labels: A Adj SN V Adv or **A Adj Adj SN V Adv Adv**			
Sentence Examples: 1. The sleepy puppies yawned noisily.		2. The two excited puppies barked loudly today.	
Sentence Checklist: 1. Did you follow the labels? 2. Did you use the words in the Word Bank?		3. Did you check for the five sentence parts? 4. Did you write neatly?	

© SHURLEY INSTRUCTIONAL MATERIALS, INC.

Reference 7: A and An Choices

Rule 1: Use the word ***a*** when the next word begins with a consonant sound. (*Example: a tree*)
Rule 2: Use the word ***an*** when the next word begins with a vowel sound. (*Example: an orange*)

Sample Sentences: Write ***a*** or ***an*** in the blanks.

1. David saw __**an**__ old eagle.
2. David saw __**a**__ young eagle.
3. The chef baked __**a**__ pie.
4. The chef baked __**an**__ apple pie.

Reference 8: Preposition and Object of the Preposition

SN V P A OP
Sam fell down the hill.

In the sample sentence, *Sam fell **down the hill***, the word *down* is a preposition because it has the noun *hill* after it that answers the question **what**. To find the preposition and object of the preposition in the Question and Answer Flow, say:

down - Preposition
down what? hill - Object of the Preposition

Reference 9: Parts-of-Speech Word Bank With Prepositional Phrases

On notebook paper, write a sentence using the words in the Word Bank. Put the words you select in the same order as the Sentence Labels listed below. Write the correct label above each word in your sentence.

WORD BANK

Nouns	Verbs	Adjectives	Adverbs	Prepositional Phrases
children dogs otters	swam splashed played	a, an, the, four, several, young, brown, happy, excited	gracefully, playfully, joyfully, happily, merrily, loudly	in the water on the beach by the trees

Sentence Labels: A Adj SN V Adv Prep Phrase or **Adj SN V Adv Prep Phrase**

Examples:

1. Several children played merrily on the beach.
2. Four otters swam playfully in the water.
3. The young dogs splashed loudly in the water.
4. The brown dogs played happily by the trees.
5. The excited children splashed loudly in the water.
6. Several otters swam gracefully by the trees.

© SHURLEY INSTRUCTIONAL MATERIALS, INC.

Reference 10: Knowing the Difference Between Prepositions and Adverbs

In the sample sentence, *Sam fell* ***down***, the word *down* is an adverb because it tells where and does not have a noun after it.

In the sample sentence, *Sam fell* ***down the hill***, the word *down* is a preposition because it has the noun *hill* after it that answers the question **what**. To find the preposition and object of the preposition in the Question and Answer Flow, say:

down - Preposition
down what? hill - Object of the Preposition

Reference 11: Capitalization Rules

1. Capitalize the first word of a sentence.
2. Capitalize the pronoun I.
3. Capitalize the names of people. (*Kelly, Billy*)
4. Capitalize the days of the week. (*Monday, Tuesday*)
5. Capitalize the months of the year. (*March, April*)
6. Capitalize the names of cities. (*Dallas*)
7. Capitalize the names of states. (*Missouri*)

Examples

Directions: Correct each capitalization mistake and write the rule number above the corrections. Put a (.) or a (?) at the end of each sentence.

1 **(capitalization rule numbers)**
T
1. the big dog barked loudly **.** **(1 capital)**

1 (or 2) **4** **5** **(capitalization rule numbers)**
I **F** **J**
4. i worked one friday in june **.** **(3 capitals)**

1 **2** **(capitalization rule numbers)**
M **I**
2. may i play here **?** **(2 capitals)**

1 **3** **6** **7** **(capitalization rule numbers)**
W **J** **O** **F**
5. we talked to jim in orlando, florida **.** **(4 capitals)**

1 **3** **(capitalization rule numbers)**
H **T**
3. he ran to tommy **.** **(2 capitals)**

Reference 12: Definitions for Singular and Plural Nouns

1. A **singular noun** usually does not end in *s* or *es* and means only one. (*ship, clown, cat*)
   Exception: Some nouns that end in s are singular and mean only one. (*glass, mess, class*)
2. A **plural noun** usually ends in *s* or *es* and means more than one. (*ships, clowns, cats*)
   Exception: Some nouns are made plural by changing their spelling. (*tooth - teeth, woman - women*)

© SHURLEY INSTRUCTIONAL MATERIALS, INC.

Reference 13: Singular and Plural Nouns					
For each noun listed below, write **S** for singular or **P** for plural.					
Noun	**S or P**	**Noun**	**S or P**	**Noun**	**S or P**
1. trees	**P**	4. child	**S**	7. shoes	**P**
2. tooth	**S**	5. teeth	**P**	8. children	**P**
3. frog	**S**	6. bus	**S**	9. tiger	**S**

Reference 14: Definitions for Common and Proper Nouns

1. A **common noun** names ANY person, place, or thing. A common noun is not capitalized because it does not name a specific person, place, or thing. (*trees, lake*)
2. A **proper noun** is a noun that names a specific, or particular, person, place, or thing. Proper nouns are always capitalized no matter where they are located in the sentence. (*Matthew, Hawaii*)

Reference 15: Common and Proper Nouns					
For each noun listed below, write **C** for common or **P** for proper.					
Noun	**C or P**	**Noun**	**C or P**	**Noun**	**C or P**
1. Christmas	**P**	4. Texas	**P**	7. Denver	**P**
2. jar	**C**	5. Sam	**P**	8. coat	**C**
3. nurse	**C**	6. horse	**C**	9. girl	**C**

Reference 16: Sample Vocabulary Words for Practice and Improved Sentences

Nouns		Verbs	Adjectives	Adverbs	Prepositions
boys	girls	laughed	a, an, the	quietly	across
brother	sailor	raced	hungry	quickly	at
cars	ship	walked	red	happily	down
horse	bears	sat	three	today	in
mother	father	jumped	friendly	loudly	on
monkeys	bees	sailed	angry	slowly	to
cats	dogs	climbed	happy	noisily	by
students	airplane	flew	sleepy	yesterday	

© SHURLEY INSTRUCTIONAL MATERIALS, INC.

Reference 17: The Topic		
Finding the topic: Write the name of the topic that best describes what each column of words is about. Choose from these topics: **Trees** **Colors** **Animals** **Books** **Holidays**.		
(1) **Animals**	(2) **Holidays**	(3) **Colors**
squirrel	Thanksgiving	purple
raccoon	Easter	black
rabbit	Christmas	yellow

Reference 18: Supporting and Non-Supporting Ideas		
Words and ideas that support the topic: In each column, cross out the one word or idea that does not support the underlined topic at the top.		
(1) **Zoo Animals**	(2) **Fruit**	(3) **Numbers**
monkey	apple	four
elephant	banana	~~**jelly**~~
tiger	~~**wheat**~~	nine
~~**umbrella**~~	peach	seven

Reference 19: Supporting and Non-Supporting Sentences

Sentences that support the topic: Read the topic. Then, cross out the one sentence that does not support the topic.

Topic: My New Tree House

1. My dad built a tree house for my birthday.
2. My tree house is way up in an oak tree.
3. ~~**My dad gave me a bat for Christmas.**~~
4. My friends come over, and we play in my new tree house.

© SHURLEY INSTRUCTIONAL MATERIALS, INC.

Reference 20: Two-Point Expository Paragraph Example

List of colors: red, blue, green, yellow, white, orange, brown, black, pink, gray, and purple.

Topic: **My Favorite colors**
Two main points: 1. **orange** 2. **green**

Sentence #1 – Topic Sentence (*Use words in the topic and tell how many points will be used.*)
I have two favorite colors.

Sentence #2 – Two-Point Sentence (*List the 2 points in the order you will present them.*)
These colors are orange and green.

Sentence #3 – First Point
My first favorite color is orange.

Sentence #4 – Supporting Sentence for the first point.
I like orange because my pet goldfish is a bright shade of orange.

Sentence #5 – Second Point
My second favorite color is green.

Sentence #6 – Supporting Sentence for the second point.
Green makes me think of grass, leaves, and going outside to play in the summertime.

Sentence #7 – Concluding (final) Sentence. (*Restate the topic sentence and add an extra thought.*)
My two favorite colors make me happy because they remind me of fun things.

SAMPLE PARAGRAPH My Favorite Colors

I have two favorite colors. These colors are orange and green. My first favorite color is orange. I like orange because my pet goldfish is a bright shade of orange. My second favorite color is green. Green makes me think of grass, leaves, and going outside to play in the summertime. My two favorite colors make me happy because they remind me of fun things.

General Checklist: Check the Finished Paragraph	The Two-Point Expository Paragraph Outline
(1) Have you followed the pattern for a two-point paragraph? (*Indent, topic sentence, 2-point sentence, 2 main points, 2 supporting sentences, and a concluding sentence.*)	Topic 2 points about the topic Sentence #1: **Topic** sentence Sentence #2: A **two-point** sentence
(2) Do you have complete sentences?	Sentence #3: A **first-point** sentence Sentence #4: A **supporting** sentence for the first point
(3) Have you capitalized the first word and put an end mark at the end of every sentence?	Sentence #5: A **second-point** sentence Sentence #6: A **supporting** sentence for the second point
(4) Have you checked your sentences for capitalization and end-mark mistakes?	Sentence #7: A **concluding** sentence

© SHURLEY INSTRUCTIONAL MATERIALS, INC.

Reference 21: Paragraph for Singular and Plural Points

Two-Point Expository Paragraph

Topic: My favorite animals
2-points: 1. beavers 2. otters

I have two favorite animals. These animals are beavers and otters. My first favorite animal is a beaver. I think watching beavers build a dam across a river is very fascinating. My second favorite animal is an otter. I like otters because they are so funny when they play in the water. My two favorite animals are fun to watch at work and at play.

Reference 22: Complete Sentences and Sentence Fragments

Identifying complete sentences and sentence fragments: Write **S** for a complete sentence and **F** for a sentence fragment on the line beside each group of words below.

S	1. The fish were swimming around in the aquarium.
F	2. For a few dollars.
S	3. The replacement part arrived yesterday.
S	4. George laughed.
F	5. Played during the recital.
F	6. The peaches on the trees.

Reference 23: Matching Subject Parts and Predicate Parts

Match each subject part with the correct predicate part by writing the correct sentence number in the blank.

1.	The purple crayon	**3**	climbed to the top of the tree.
2.	A white truck	**1**	broke in half.
3.	Two black cats	**4**	hurt my eyes.
4.	The bright light	**2**	parked in front of the store.

Reference 24: Contractions

isn't **is not**	**aren't** **are not**	**wasn't** **was not**	**weren't** **were not**
The pen **is not** here.	The books **are not** new.	The cat **was not** outside.	The boys **were not** early.
The pen **isn't** here.	The books **aren't** new.	The cat **wasn't** outside.	The boys **weren't** early.

© SHURLEY INSTRUCTIONAL MATERIALS, INC.

Reference 25: More Contractions				
I'm I am	**can't cannot**	**don't do not**	**doesn't does not**	**didn't did not**
I am not home.	You **cannot** go.	We **do not** see you.	The man **does not** hear.	I **did not** know.
I'm not home.	You **can't** go.	We **don't** see you.	The man **doesn't** hear.	I **didn't** know.

Reference 26: Present, Past, and Future Verb Tenses

When you are writing paragraphs, you must use verbs that are in the same tense. **Tense** means time. The tense of a verb shows the time of the action. There are three basic tenses that show when an action takes place. They are **past tense, present tense,** and **future tense**. Now, you will learn to recognize each kind of tense.

1. The **past tense** shows that something has happened sometime in the past. Most past tense verbs are made past tense by adding an **-ed** to the end of the word. If a verb uses **-ed** to make the past tense form, it is called a **regular** past tense verb: listen-**listened,** talk-**talked,** play-**played,** jump-**jumped**.

   Other past tense verbs are made past tense by changing their **spelling form** and not by adding **-ed**. If a verb uses a spelling change to make the past tense form, it is called an **irregular** past tense verb: give-**gave,** take-**took,** sell-**sold,** buy-**bought.** *(The verbs are listed as regular or irregular for you.)*

2. The **present tense** shows that something is happening now, in the present. Present tense verbs can end with an **-s** for singular subjects or without an **-s** for plural subjects: **listens-listen, talks-talk, plays-play, jumps-jump, gives-give, takes-take, sells-sell, buys-buy.** *(The verbs are listed as regular or irregular for you.)*

3. The **future tense** shows that something will happen at some time in the future. The future tense form always has the helping verb *will* before the main verb. Future tense verb examples: **will talk, will listen, will play, will jump, will see, will give, will take, will sell, will buy.**

Example: Identify the tense of each underlined verb by writing a number **1** for past tense, a number **2** for present tense, or a number **3** for future tense.

Verb Tense	Regular Verbs	Verb Tense	Irregular Verbs
1	1. She listened to the radio.	**2**	4. Larry sells used cars.
2	2. She listens to the radio.	**1**	5. Larry sold used cars.
3	3. She will listen to the radio.	**3**	6. Larry will sell used cars.

© SHURLEY INSTRUCTIONAL MATERIALS, INC.

Reference 27: Tips for Writing Friendly Letters

Tip #1: Write as if you were talking to the person face-to-face. Share information about yourself and mutual friends. Tell stories, conversations, or jokes. Share pictures, articles, drawings, poems, etc. Avoid saying something about someone else that you'll be sorry for later.

Tip #2: If you are writing a return letter, be sure to answer any questions that were asked. Repeat the question so that your reader will know what you are writing about. (You asked about . . .)

Tip #3: End your letter in a positive way so that your reader will want to write a return letter.

Reference 28: Friendly Letter Example

1. Heading

Write your address.
Write the date.

23 Circle Drive
Dallas, TX 93312
April 3, 20____

2. Friendly Greeting

Name the person receiving the letter.
Use a comma.

Dear Jonathan,

3. Body (Indent Paragraphs)

Write what you want to say. Indent.

Are you playing baseball again this year? I would really like to come to watch one of your games. Please let me know when your season begins.

4. Closing

Capitalize the first word.
Use a comma.

Your cousin,

5. Signature

Sign your name.

Timothy

© SHURLEY INSTRUCTIONAL MATERIALS, INC.

Reference 29: Thank-You Note for a Gift

What - Thank you for...
(tell color, kind, and item)
Use - Tell how the gift is used.
Thanks - I appreciate your thinking of me at this time.

Example 1: Gift

Heading

3132 Apple Street
Greenwood, KS 15023
June 3, 20____

Greeting

Dear Mrs. Smith,

Body

Thank you for the book about sea animals. It has been a wonderful research tool for my science project. Thank you for your kindness.

Closing

Sincerely,

Signature

Elizabeth

Reference 30: Thank-You Note for an Action

What - Thank you for...
(tell action)
Use - Tell how the action helped.
Thanks - I appreciate your remembering me.

Example 2: Action

Heading

239 Bluebird Lane
Charleston, SC 99173
August 1, 20____

Greeting

Dear Linda,

Body

Thank you for visiting me in the hospital. I was so thrilled to see a familiar face. I appreciate your kindness.

Closing

Your friend,

Signature

Kathleen

© SHURLEY INSTRUCTIONAL MATERIALS, INC.

Reference 31: Alphabetical Order

Directions: Put each group of words in alphabetical order. Use numbers to show the order in each column.

Animal Words	"G" Words	Farm Words	Color Words	"L" Words
2 1. rabbit	2 3. garden	1 5. barn	1 7. black	2 9. light
1 2. donkey	1 4. game	2 6. tractor	2 8. blue	1 10. leg

Reference 32: Three Main Parts of the Library

Fiction Section
Fiction books contain stories about people, places, or things that are not true.

Nonfiction Section
Nonfiction books contain information and stories that are true.

Reference Section
The Reference Section is designed to help you find information on many topics. The most common reference books are the dictionary and the encyclopedia.

Reference 33: "Piggy Under the Fence"

In the barnyard lived a cute little pig named Piggy. Piggy loved to crawl under the fence. Piggy said, "Under, under, under. Under the fence. My! My! My! I LOVE to crawl under the fence!"

First, the farmer caught Piggy crawling under the fence. The farmer said, "Under, under, under. Under the fence. My! My! My! Piggy LOVES to crawl under the fence! I do not know what to do."

Next, the farmer's wife caught Piggy crawling under the fence. The farmer's wife said, "Under, under, under. Under the fence. My! My! My! Piggy LOVES to crawl under the fence! I do not know what to do."

Then, the farmer's children caught Piggy crawling under the fence. The farmer's children said, "Under, under, under. Under the fence. My! My! My! Piggy LOVES to crawl under the fence! We do not know what to do."

But Piggy's mother did not smile. Piggy's mother said, "Under, under, under. Under the fence. My! My! My! I know what to do. If Piggy crawls under the fence again, Piggy will go over my knee!"

Piggy looked at the fence. Piggy looked at his mother. Then, Piggy said, "Under, under, under. Under the fence. My! My! My! I do NOT like to crawl under the fence anymore!"

© SHURLEY INSTRUCTIONAL MATERIALS, INC.

Notes

© SHURLEY INSTRUCTIONAL MATERIALS, INC.

PRACTICE

SECTION

Chapter 10, Lesson 1, Practice: Classify the sentence below. Use **SN** for subject noun, **V** for verb, **Adv** for adverb, **Adj** for adjective, and **A** for article adjective. Underline the complete subject one time and the complete predicate two times.

The seven white rabbits hopped quickly away.

Chapter 10, Lesson 2, Practice: Classify the sentence below. Use **SN** for subject noun, **V** for verb, **Adv** for adverb, **Adj** for adjective, and **A** for article adjective. Underline the complete subject one time and the complete predicate two times.

The three young actors bowed gracefully.

Chapter 10, Lesson 3, Practice: Classify the sentence below. Use **SN** for subject noun, **V** for verb, **Adv** for adverb, **Adj** for adjective, and **A** for article adjective. Underline the complete subject one time and the complete predicate two times.

The two busy children played happily today.

Chapter 11, Lesson 1, Practice 1: On notebook paper, write each sentence correctly. Capitalize the first word of each sentence and put a (.) or a (**?**) at the end.

1. did the car lights dim suddenly
2. the chocolate cake baked slowly
3. the hungry baby cried softly
4. the school telephone rang loudly

© SHURLEY INSTRUCTIONAL MATERIALS, INC.

Chapter 11, Lesson 1, Practice 2: On notebook paper, write a sentence using the words in the Word Bank. Put the words you select in the same order as the Sentence Labels listed below. Write the correct label above each word in your sentence.

WORD BANK

Nouns	Verbs	Adjectives	Adverbs
babies puppies toddlers	whined, cried, yawned, played, smiled, crawled, napped	a, an, the, two, tiny, upset, hungry, excited, three, pretty, unhappy, sleepy	swiftly, softly, loudly, quietly, happily, noisily, yesterday

Sentence Labels: A Adj SN V Adv (Bonus) A Adj Adj SN V Adv Adv

Chapter 11, Lesson 2, Practice 1: On notebook paper, write each sentence correctly. Capitalize the first word of each sentence and put a (.) or a (?) at the end.

1. an orange ball bounced slowly
2. was the sun shining brightly
3. the bananas ripened quickly
4. the bees buzzed wildly

Chapter 11, Lesson 2, Practice 2: On notebook paper, write a sentence using the words in the Word Bank. Put the words you select in the same order as the Sentence Labels listed below. Write the correct label above each word in your sentence.

WORD BANK

Nouns	Verbs	Adjectives	Adverbs
bats sparrows owls	dove, swooped, flew, landed	a, an, the, three, swift, hungry, old, young, brown, black	carelessly, dangerously, low, high, today

Sentence Labels: A Adj SN V Adv (Bonus) A Adj Adj SN V Adv Adv

© SHURLEY INSTRUCTIONAL MATERIALS, INC.

Chapter 11, Lesson 3, Practice 1: On notebook paper, write each sentence correctly. Capitalize the first word of each sentence and put a (.) or a (?) at the end.

1. the excited fans cheered loudly
2. did the glass window crack yesterday
3. do bankers work tomorrow
4. the wheat bread baked slowly

Chapter 11, Lesson 3, Practice 2: On notebook paper, write a sentence using the words in the Word Bank. Put the words you select in the same order as the Sentence Labels listed below. Write the correct label above each word in your sentence.

WORD BANK

Nouns	Verbs	Adjectives	Adverbs
flowers, buds, grass, trees	bloomed, opened, grew, wilted	a, an, the, four, colorful, bright, new, green, yellow, red, large	quickly, rapidly, slowly, today, beautifully, yesterday

Sentence Labels: A Adj Adj SN V Adv Adv

Chapter 12, Lesson 1, Practice 1: Write ***a*** or ***an*** in the blanks.

1. _____ awful storm frightened me.
2. Columbus was _____ explorer.
3. The workers dug _____ hole.
4. Jim found _____ empty can.
5. _____ alarm
6. _____ scarf
7. _____ case
8. _____ acorn

© SHURLEY INSTRUCTIONAL MATERIALS, INC.

Chapter 12, Lesson 1, Practice 2: On notebook paper, write a sentence using the words in the Word Bank. Put the words you select in the same order as the Sentence Labels listed below. Write the correct label above each word in your sentence.

WORD BANK

Nouns	Verbs	Adjectives	Adverbs
birds rabbits grasshoppers	hopped, jumped, sat, nibbled, played, hid	a, an, the, cute, three, baby, brown, green, white, gentle, funny, small, shy	merrily, quietly, excitedly, noisily, yesterday, swiftly, slowly, rapidly

Sentence Labels: A Adj SN V Adv (Bonus) A Adj Adj SN V Adv Adv

Chapter 12, Lesson 2, Practice 1: Write ***a*** or ***an*** in the blanks.

1. The king built _____ castle.
2. She pointed to _____ exit.
3. Our group had _____ guide.
4. _____ elephant looked at me.
5. _____ inch
6. _____ hat
7. _____ hallway
8. _____ elk

Chapter 12, Lesson 2, Practice 2: On notebook paper, write a sentence using the words in the Word Bank. Put the words you select in the same order as the Sentence Labels listed below. Write the correct label above each word in your sentence.

WORD BANK

Nouns	Verbs	Adjectives	Adverbs
duck swan eagle	glided, flew, soared, landed, floated, swam, ran, ate	a, an, the, one, white, large, baby, beautiful, brown, strong, brave, loud, small	gracefully, quietly, rapidly, swiftly, high, far, away, gently, today, loudly, softly

Sentence Labels: A Adj SN V Adv (Bonus) A Adj Adj SN V Adv Adv

© SHURLEY INSTRUCTIONAL MATERIALS, INC.

Chapter 12, Lesson 3, Practice 1: Write ***a*** or ***an*** in the blanks.

1. A gorilla is _____ animal.
2. The man carried _____ package.
3. Dad bought _____ computer.
4. She bought _____ extra suitcase.
5. _____ apron
6. _____ lemon
7. _____ ruler
8. _____ office

Chapter 12, Lesson 3, Practice 2: On notebook paper, write a sentence using the words in the Word Bank. Put the words you select in the same order as the Sentence Labels listed below. Write the correct label above each word in your sentence.

WORD BANK

Nouns	Verbs	Adjectives	Adverbs
cows horses goats	grazed, drank, walked, stood, ran, ate, worked, chewed, slept, kicked	a, an, the, two, black, lazy, old, brown, young, small, large, smart, frightened	calmly, excitedly, fast, happily, noisily, quietly, today, daily, soundly, hard

Sentence Labels: A Adj SN V Adv (Bonus) A Adj Adj SN V Adv Adv

Chapter 14, Lesson 2, Practice 1: Write ***a*** or ***an*** in the blanks.

1. The farmer drove _____ tractor.
2. Pat read _____ adventure story.
3. He drove _____ new car.
4. Sara picked _____ red rose.
5. _____ alligator
6. _____ elbow
7. _____ candle
8. _____ orange

© SHURLEY INSTRUCTIONAL MATERIALS, INC.

Chapter 14, Lesson 2, Practice 2: On notebook paper, write a sentence using the words in the Word Bank. Put the words you select in the same order as the Sentence Labels listed below. Write the correct label above each word in your sentence.

WORD BANK

Nouns	Verbs	Adjectives	Adverbs	Prepositional Phrases
students children soldiers	talked, chatted, whispered, laughed	a, an, the, four, young, excited, busy, happy, lazy, little, silly, shy, tired	quietly cautiously secretly noisily	on the telephone across the table by the store in the restaurant

Sentence Labels: A Adj Adj SN V Adv Prep Phrase

Chapter 14, Lesson 3, Practice 1: On notebook paper, write a sentence using the words in the Word Bank. Put the words you select in the same order as the Sentence Labels listed below. Write the correct label above each word in your sentence.

WORD BANK

Nouns	Verbs	Adjectives	Adverbs	Prepositional Phrases
mouse squirrel raccoons	jumped moved ran	a, an, the, old, brown, young, three, eager,	loudly, quickly, noisily, silently, slowly, today	down the road across the yard on the porch

Sentence Labels: A Adj Adj SN V Adv Prep Phrase

Chapter 14, Lesson 3, Practice 2: Classify the sentence below. Use **SN** for subject noun, **V** for verb, **Adv** for adverb, **Adj** for adjective, **A** for article adjective, **P** for preposition, and **OP** for object of the preposition. Underline the complete subject <u>one</u> time and the complete predicate <u>two</u> times.

The little yellow ducks swam happily in the pond.

© SHURLEY INSTRUCTIONAL MATERIALS, INC.

Chapter 15, Lesson 1, Practice: Correct the capitalization mistakes and put the rule number above each correction. Use the rule numbers in Reference 11 on page 17 in the Reference Section of your book. Put a (.) or a (?) at the end of the sentence.

_____ **(capitalization rule numbers)**

alice wrote a letter to julie on thursday _____ **(3 capitals)**

Chapter 15, Lesson 2, Practice: Correct the capitalization mistakes and put the rule number above each correction. Use the rule numbers in Reference 11 on page 17 in the Reference Section of your book. Put a (.) or a (?) at the end of the sentence.

_____ **(capitalization rule numbers)**

timothy moved to tucson, arizona, last july _____ **(4 capitals)**

Chapter 15, Lesson 3, Practice 1: Correct the capitalization mistakes and put the rule number above each correction. Use the rule numbers in Reference 11 on page 17 in the Reference Section of your book. Put a (.) or a (?) at the end of the sentence.

_____ **(capitalization rule numbers)**

1. may i visit mary on wednesday _____ **(4 capitals)**

_____ **(capitalization rule numbers)**

2. chris lives in seattle, washington _____ **(3 capitals)**

© SHURLEY INSTRUCTIONAL MATERIALS, INC.

Chapter 15, Lesson 3, Practice 2: On notebook paper, write a sentence using the words in the Word Bank. Put the words you select in the same order as the Sentence Labels listed below. Write the correct label above each word in your sentence.

WORD BANK

Nouns	Verbs	Adjectives	Adverbs	Prepositional Phrases
wind breeze storm	blew gusted howled	a, an, the, cold, refreshing, hot, severe, spring, soft, gentle, harsh, dark, summer, winter	loudly, strongly, suddenly, today, calmly, silently, yesterday	across the lake at night in the tunnel during the day in the mountains

Sentence Labels: A Adj SN V Adv Prep Phrase

Independent Exercise: Choose your own Sentence Labels.

Chapter 16, Lesson 1, Practice: For each noun listed below, write **S** for singular or **P** for plural.

Noun	S or P	Noun	S or P	Noun	S or P
1. bears		5. ants		9. cars	
2. goose		6. balloon		10. geese	
3. babies		7. feet		11. church	
4. dog		8. foot		12. windows	

Chapter 16, Lesson 2, Practice: For each noun listed below, write **S** for singular or **P** for plural.

Noun	S or P	Noun	S or P	Noun	S or P
1. sleds		5. women		9. turtles	
2. flower		6. horse		10. mice	
3. kittens		7. clowns		11. foxes	
4. mouse		8. crib		12. pig	

© SHURLEY INSTRUCTIONAL MATERIALS, INC.

Chapter 16, Lesson 3, Practice 1: For each noun listed below, write **S** for singular or **P** for plural.

Noun	S or P	Noun	S or P	Noun	S or P
1. rabbits		5. families		9. ducks	
2. airplane		6. kite		10. men	
3. monkeys		7. trains		11. bird	
4. man		8. butterfly		12. doll	

Chapter 16, Lesson 3, Practice 2: Correct the capitalization mistakes and put the rule number above each correction. Use the rule numbers in Reference 11 on page 17 in the Reference Section of your book. Put a (**.**) or a (**?**) at the end of the sentence.

_____**(capitalization rule numbers)**

i am leaving on monday for chicago, illinois _____ **(4 capitals)**

Chapter 16, Lesson 3, Practice 3: On notebook paper, write a sentence using the words in the Word Bank. Put the words you select in the same order as the Sentence Labels listed below. Write the correct label above each word in your sentence.

WORD BANK

Nouns	Verbs	Adjectives	Adverbs	Prepositional Phrases
airplane helicopter jet	landed arrived flew	a, an, the, large, loud, new, swift, fast, big, blue, silver, army	promptly, carefully, safely, today, suddenly, around, rapidly	on time at the airport on the runway to the ship

Sentence Labels: A Adj SN V Adv Prep Phrase

Independent Exercise: Choose your own Sentence Labels.

© SHURLEY INSTRUCTIONAL MATERIALS, INC.

Chapter 17, Lesson 1, Practice: For each noun listed below, write **C** for common or **P** for proper.

Noun	C or P	Noun	C or P	Noun	C or P
1. student		5. Ted		9. Easter	
2. Mr. Smith		6. England		10. cup	
3. city		7. boy		11. clock	
4. Kansas		8. Italy		12. map	

Chapter 17, Lesson 2, Practice: For each noun listed below, write **C** for common or **P** for proper.

Noun	C or P	Noun	C or P	Noun	C or P
1. Walker School		5. watch		9. Anna	
2. Mandy		6. cloud		10. mail	
3. milk		7. Mr. Jones		11. state	
4. tiger		8. August		12. Thanksgiving	

Chapter 17, Lesson 3, Practice 1: For each noun listed below, write **C** for common or **P** for proper.

Noun	C or P	Noun	C or P	Noun	C or P
1. cake		5. Monday		9. July	
2. Mr. Brown		6. James		10. Africa	
3. duck		7. key		11. Tuesday	
4. January		8. barn		12. desk	

© SHURLEY INSTRUCTIONAL MATERIALS, INC.

Chapter 17, Lesson 3, Practice 2: For each noun listed below, write **S** for singular or **P** for plural.

Noun	S or P	Noun	S or P	Noun	S or P
1. friends		5. prunes		9. leg	
2. bug		6. games		10. arm	
3. stars		7. house		11. knee	
4. bushes		8. street		12. letters	

Chapter 17, Lesson 3, Practice 3: Correct the capitalization mistakes and put the rule number above each correction. Use the rule numbers in Reference 11 on page 17 in the Reference Section of your book. Put a (**.**) or a (**?**) at the end of the sentence.

_____ **(capitalization rule numbers)**

peter will arrive in oregon next tuesday _____ **(3 capitals)**

Chapter 18, Lesson 1, Practice 1: Write the name of the topic that best describes what each column of words is about. Choose from these topics:

Colors **City Things** **Animals** **Country Things** **Shapes**

(1)	(2)	(3)
_____	_____	_____
skyscraper	tractor	triangle
taxi	farm	square
subway	barn	circle

© SHURLEY INSTRUCTIONAL MATERIALS, INC.

Chapter 18, Lesson 1, Practice 2: In each column, cross out the one idea that does not support the underlined topic at the top.

(1) **Kitchen Things**	(2) **Breakfast**	(3) **Birds**
skillet	cereal	hawk
umpire	toast	eagle
oven	eggs	rat
spoon	automobile	robin

Chapter 18, Lesson 1, Practice 3: Read each topic. Then, cross out the one sentence that does not support the topic.

A. Topic: My Dog Buddy

1. My dog's name is Buddy.
2. Buddy likes to play fetch.
3. Buddy sleeps beside my bed at night.
4. My horse's name is Flash.

B. Topic: Summer Vacation

1. My family takes a vacation every summer.
2. This summer we are going to Hawaii.
3. We visited Grandmother on Thanksgiving.
4. Last summer, we went to Florida.

Chapter 18, Lesson 2, Practice 1: Correct the capitalization mistakes and put the rule number above each correction. Use the rule numbers in Reference 11 on page 17 in the Reference Section of your book. Put a (**.**) or a (**?**) at the end of the sentence.

_____ **(capitalization rule numbers)**

stephen and billy will travel to atlanta in february ____ **(4 capitals)**

© SHURLEY INSTRUCTIONAL MATERIALS, INC.

Chapter 18, Lesson 2, Practice 2: Write the name of the topic that best describes what each column of words is about. Choose from these topics:

Colors **Transportation** **Farm Animals** **Kitchen Things** **Green Things**

(1)	(2)	(3)
_____	_____	_____
leaf	car	goat
grasshopper	truck	pig
grass	van	cow

Chapter 18, Lesson 2, Practice 3: In each column, cross out the one idea that does not support the underlined topic at the top.

(1) **Flowers**	(2) **Clothing**	(3) **Yellow Things**
rose	socks	banana
ocean	pants	school bus
daisy	skirt	lake
tulip	lamp	lemon

Chapter 18, Lesson 2, Practice 4: Read each topic. Then, cross out the one sentence that does not support the topic.

A. Topic: The Library

1. The library is full of wonderful books.
2. The library is open six days a week.
3. I like to borrow many books from the library.
4. I need to go grocery shopping today.

B. Topic: A Day at the Lake

1. Every summer, we spend a day at the lake.
2. We rent a boat early in the morning.
3. My brother got a new computer.
4. My dad and I ski behind the boat.

© SHURLEY INSTRUCTIONAL MATERIALS, INC.

Chapter 18, Lesson 3, Practice 1: Write the name of the topic that best describes what each column of words is about. Choose from these topics:

Colors **Winter Things** **Ocean Animals** **Yellow Things** **Summer Things**

(1)	(2)	(3)
_____	_____	_____
gloves	dolphin	sun
coat	whale	butter
snow	shark	corn

Chapter 18, Lesson 3, Practice 2: In each column, cross out the one idea that does not support the underlined topic at the top.

(1) **People**	(2) **States**	(3) **Farm Words**
police officer	Nevada	tractor
hippopotamus	Louisiana	plow
teacher	Vermont	plastic
mother	cheese	barn

Chapter 18, Lesson 3, Practice 3: Read each topic. Then, cross out the one sentence that does not support the topic.

A. Topic: Uncle David

1. Uncle David works on a farm.
2. Uncle David lives in Oklahoma.
3. Uncle David is my favorite uncle.
4. Aunt Rita works in a clothing factory.

B. Topic: Our House

1. We live in a small white house.
2. Our house is on Elm Street.
3. Joey lives in Dallas.
4. We have lived in our house for ten years.

© SHURLEY INSTRUCTIONAL MATERIALS, INC.

Chapter 18, Lesson 3, Practice 4: Correct the capitalization mistakes and put the rule number above each correction. Use the rule numbers in Reference 11 on page 17 in the Reference Section of your book. Put a (**.**) or a (**?**) at the end of the sentence.

_____ **(capitalization rule numbers)**

jack will bring punch and cookies on wednesday night ____ **(2 capitals)**

Chapter 18, Lesson 3, Practice 5: On notebook paper, write a sentence using the words in the Word Bank. Put the words you select in the same order as the Sentence Labels listed below. Write the correct label above each word in your sentence.

WORD BANK

Nouns	Verbs	Adjectives	Adverbs	Prepositional Phrases
clown kite balloon friend	waved, shouted, soared, talked, floated, walked	a, an, the, silly, large, funny, best, old, new, giant, happy, green, silly	eagerly, high, excitedly, often, silently, loudly, today	to the children in the sky to the mall to the crowd

Sentence Labels: A Adj Adj SN V Adv Prep Phrase

Independent Exercise: Choose your own Sentence Labels and Words.

Chapter 18, Lesson 4, Practice 1: Write the name of the topic that best describes what each column of words is about. Choose from these topics:

Numbers **Table Things** **Animals** **Weather Words** **Drinks**

(1)	(2)	(3)
_____	_____	_____
cloudy	eight	punch
rainy	two	soda
windy	three	juice

© SHURLEY INSTRUCTIONAL MATERIALS, INC.

Chapter 18, Lesson 4, Practice 2: In each column, cross out the one idea that does not support the underlined topic at the top.

(1) **Brown Things**	(2) **Beans**	(3) **Vegetables**
dirt	refried	carrots
sky	green	squash
chocolate	pinto	gravy
otter	mail	broccoli

Chapter 18, Lesson 4, Practice 3: Read each topic. Then, cross out the one sentence that does not support the topic.

A. Topic: Happiness

1. Happiness is being with my mom.
2. Happiness is a warm hug.
3. Happiness is a beautiful rainbow.
4. Scary movies frighten me.

B. Topic: My New Shoes

1. My new shoes are white.
2. My new shoes feel comfortable on my feet.
3. My old shoes were black.
4. My new shoes have purple laces.

Chapter 18, Lesson 4, Practice 4: Correct the capitalization mistakes and put the rule number above each correction. Use the rule numbers in Reference 11 on page 17 in the Reference Section of your book. Put a (**.**) or a (**?**) at the end of the sentence.

_____ **(capitalization rule numbers)**

may i have another piece of janet's pie ____ **(3 capitals)**

© SHURLEY INSTRUCTIONAL MATERIALS, INC.

Chapter 19, Lesson 1, Practice: Use Writing Outline 1 for Writing Assignment #1. Use this two-point outline form to guide you as you write a two-point expository paragraph.

Writing Outline 1

Write a topic: _____

Write 2 points to list about the topic.

1._____ 2._____

Sentence #1 Topic sentence (*Use words in the topic and tell how many points will be used.*)

_____

_____

Sentence #2 2-point sentence (*List your 2 points in the order that you will present them.*)

_____

_____

Sentence #3 State your first point in a complete sentence.

_____

_____

Sentence #4 Write a supporting sentence for the first point.

_____

_____

Sentence #5 State your second point in a complete sentence.

_____

_____

Sentence #6 Write a supporting sentence for the second point.

_____

_____

Sentence #7 Concluding sentence (*Restate the topic sentence and add an extra thought.*)

_____

_____

© SHURLEY INSTRUCTIONAL MATERIALS, INC.

Chapter 19, Lesson 4, Practice: Use Writing Outline 2 for Writing Assignment #2. Use this two-point outline form to guide you as you write a two-point expository paragraph.

Writing Outline 2

Write a topic: _____

Write 2 points to list about the topic.

1._____ 2._____

Sentence #1 Topic sentence (*Use words in the topic and tell how many points will be used.*)

_____

_____

Sentence #2 2-point sentence (*List your 2 points in the order that you will present them.*)

_____

_____

Sentence #3 State your first point in a complete sentence.

_____

_____

Sentence #4 Write a supporting sentence for the first point.

_____

_____

Sentence #5 State your second point in a complete sentence.

_____

_____

Sentence #6 Write a supporting sentence for the second point.

_____

_____

Sentence #7 Concluding sentence (*Restate the topic sentence and add an extra thought.*)

_____

_____

© SHURLEY INSTRUCTIONAL MATERIALS, INC.

Chapter 21, Lesson 1, Practice: Write **S** for a complete sentence and **F** for a sentence fragment on the line beside each group of words below.

_____ 1. The cookies baked in the oven.

_____ 2. Bells rang.

_____ 3. A brown camel.

_____ 4. That new book.

_____ 5. Watches baseball.

_____ 6. Across the street.

_____ 7. Every soldier waited for orders.

_____ 8. Tray rode his new bicycle.

_____ 9. Circled the tall tower.

_____ 10. A painted pony.

_____ 11. The driver stopped quickly.

_____ 12. At the park.

_____ 13. The children played in the yard.

_____ 14. In the end.

_____ 15. Flowers in the garden.

Chapter 21, Lesson 2, Practice 1: Match each subject part with the correct predicate part by writing the correct sentence number in the blank.

1. A horse _____ was in a new movie.
2. The wildflowers _____ was printed yesterday.
3. The newspaper _____ galloped through the pasture.
4. That actor _____ appeared above the trees.
5. The beautiful rainbow _____ bloomed in the field.

© SHURLEY INSTRUCTIONAL MATERIALS, INC.

Chapter 21, Lesson 2, Practice 2: Write **S** for a complete sentence and **F** for a sentence fragment on the line beside each group of words below.

_____ 1. A curious raccoon.

_____ 2. Travis walked to the store.

_____ 3. Lives in the alley.

_____ 4. This broken toy.

_____ 5. The soup cooked.

_____ 6. People in the stands.

_____ 7. The couple sat on the couch.

_____ 8. Jamie parked her car in the garage.

_____ 9. Five new kittens.

_____ 10. I did well on the test.

Chapter 21, Lesson 3, Practice 1: Match each subject part with the correct predicate part by writing the correct sentence number in the blank.

1. The glass vase _____ fit nicely.
2. The dentist _____ chased the robber.
3. Five police officers _____ shattered on the floor.
4. My Easter dress _____ squeezed under the fence.
5. A bunny _____ cleaned my teeth.

© SHURLEY INSTRUCTIONAL MATERIALS, INC.

Chapter 21, Lesson 3, Practice 2: Write **S** for a complete sentence and **F** for a sentence fragment on the line beside each group of words below.

_____ 1. An empty box.

_____ 2. We swam across the pool.

_____ 3. Flies a plane.

_____ 4. I talked with Susan.

_____ 5. Near the end of the road.

_____ 6. Trapped in the cave.

_____ 7. Ball rolled.

_____ 8. The rain fell hard.

_____ 9. The two churches.

_____ 10. The children ran fast.

Chapter 22, Lesson 1, Practice 1: Write the correct contraction in each blank.

1. are not _____
2. is not _____
3. was not _____
4. were not _____
5. is not _____
6. are not _____
7. were not _____
8. was not _____

Chapter 22, Lesson 1, Practice 2: Write the correct words beside each contraction.

1. aren't _____
2. isn't _____
3. wasn't _____
4. weren't _____
5. isn't _____
6. aren't _____
7. weren't _____
8. wasn't _____

© SHURLEY INSTRUCTIONAL MATERIALS, INC.

Chapter 22, Lesson 1, Practice 3: Underline the correct contraction at the right for the words that are underlined in each sentence. Use Reference 24 on page 21 to help you.

1. My crayons <u>are not</u> missing.	isn't	aren't
2. His pencil <u>is not</u> sharp.	isn't	aren't
3. The books <u>are not</u> expensive.	isn't	aren't
4. The officer <u>was not</u> here.	wasn't	weren't
5. My brother <u>was not</u> ill.	wasn't	weren't
6. My notes <u>were not</u> in order.	wasn't	weren't

Chapter 22, Lesson 1, Practice 4: Write the correct contraction in the blank for the words that are underlined in each sentence. Use Reference 24 on page 21 to help you.

1. The bread <u>was not</u> fresh. _____
2. My clothes <u>are not</u> packed. _____
3. The students <u>were not</u> on time. _____
4. The baby <u>is not</u> happy. _____

Chapter 22, Lesson 2, Practice 1: Write the correct contraction in each blank. Use Reference 25 on page 22 to help you.

1. I am _____
2. cannot _____
3. do not _____
4. does not _____
5. did not _____

© SHURLEY INSTRUCTIONAL MATERIALS, INC.

Chapter 22, Lesson 2, Practice 2: Write the correct words beside each contraction. Use Reference 25 on page 22 to help you.

1. didn't _____
2. can't _____
3. doesn't _____
4. I'm _____
5. don't _____

Chapter 22, Lesson 2, Practice 3: Write the correct contraction in the blank for the words that are underlined in each sentence. Use Reference 25 on page 22 to help you.

1. My mother knows that <u>I am</u> responsible. _____
2. Those boys <u>cannot</u> play. _____
3. The rain <u>did not</u> stop for days. _____
4. His room <u>does not</u> need to be cleaned. _____
5. The stores <u>do not</u> open today. _____

Chapter 22, Lesson 3, Practice 1: Write the correct contraction in each blank. Use the contraction references to help you. Use Reference 25 on page 22 to help you.

1. do not _____
2. cannot _____
3. were not _____
4. I am _____
5. are not _____
6. is not _____
7. did not _____
8. does not _____

Chapter 22, Lesson 3, Practice 2: Write the correct words beside each contraction. Use the contraction references to help you.

1. I'm _____
2. isn't _____
3. doesn't _____
4. wasn't _____
5. weren't _____
6. can't _____
7. didn't _____
8. aren't _____

© SHURLEY INSTRUCTIONAL MATERIALS, INC.

Chapter 22, Lesson 3, Practice 3: Write the correct contraction in the blank for the words that are underlined in each sentence. Use the contraction references to help you.

1. The machines <u>are not</u> broken. _____
2. I <u>cannot</u> play the tuba. _____
3. The students <u>did not</u> read the directions. _____
4. Harry <u>does not</u> play basketball. _____
5. The numbers <u>do not</u> make sense. _____
6. Jill knows that <u>I am</u> busy. _____
7. Kathy <u>is not</u> coming to my party. _____
8. Patrick <u>was not</u> paying attention. _____
9. The fans <u>were not</u> allowed on the field. _____

Chapter 23, Lesson 1, Practice 1: Identify the tense of each underlined verb by writing a number **1** for past tense, a number **2** for present tense, or a number **3** for future tense.

Verb Tense	Regular Verbs	Verb Tense	Irregular Verbs
	1. Kelly <u>will play</u> with her dolls.		7. The sisters <u>take</u> piano lessons.
	2. Kelly <u>played</u> with her dolls.		8. The sisters <u>will take</u> piano lessons.
	3. Kelly <u>plays</u> with her dolls.		9. The sisters <u>took</u> piano lessons.
	4. The hockey players <u>skate</u>.		10. Mary <u>buys</u> a blue dress.
	5. The hockey players <u>will skate</u>.		11. Mary <u>will buy</u> a blue dress.
	6. The hockey players <u>skated</u>.		12. Mary <u>bought</u> a blue dress.

© SHURLEY INSTRUCTIONAL MATERIALS, INC.

Chapter 23, Lesson 1, Practice 2: Chant the following verbs to hear the different tenses.

Regular Verbs			Irregular Verbs		
listened	listen	will listen	bought	buy	will buy
talked	talk	will talk	took	take	will take
skated	skate	will skate	drove	drive	will drive
played	play	will play	sold	sell	will sell

Chapter 23, Lesson 2, Practice: Identify the tense of each underlined verb by writing a number **1** for past tense, a number **2** for present tense, or a number **3** for future tense.

Verb Tense	Regular Verbs	Verb Tense	Irregular Verbs
	1. Tim <u>will jump</u> into the pool.		6. Jim <u>drives</u> to church.
	2. Tim <u>jumped</u> into the pool.		7. Jim <u>will drive</u> to church.
	3. Tim <u>jumps</u> into the pool.		8. Jim <u>drove</u> to church.
	4. Mom <u>yells</u> loudly for our team.		9. She <u>will sing</u> for a large audience.
	5. Mom <u>will yell</u> loudly for our team.		10. She <u>sings</u> for a large audience.

Chapter 23, Lesson 3, Practice: Identify the tense of each underlined verb by writing a number **1** for past tense, a number **2** for present tense, or a number **3** for future tense.

Verb Tense	Regular Verbs	Verb Tense	Irregular Verbs
	1. The truck <u>will back</u> into the ditch.		6. Grandma <u>speaks</u> softly.
	2. The truck <u>backed</u> into the ditch.		7. Grandma <u>will speak</u> softly.
	3. The truck <u>backs</u> into the ditch.		8. Grandma <u>spoke</u> softly.
	4. The planes <u>circle</u> the runway.		9. The workers <u>dig</u> a deep hole.
	5. The planes <u>will circle</u> the runway.		10. The workers <u>dug</u> a deep hole.

© SHURLEY INSTRUCTIONAL MATERIALS, INC.

Chapter 24, Lesson 1, Practice: Write the parts of a friendly letter in the correct places in the friendly letter below.

1. **Heading**
   19 Dogwood Lane
   Benton, KS 24550
   July 23, 20____
2. **Greeting**
   Dear Samuel,
3. **Closing**
   Your friend,
4. **Signature**
   Ruth
5. **Body**
   We just got back from our trip to Alaska. It was so much fun. I have so much to tell you!

Friendly Letter

Heading

_____

_____

_____

Greeting

_____

Body

_____

Closing

_____

Signature

_____

Chapter 24, Lesson 2, Practice 1: Identify the tense of each underlined verb by writing a number **1** for past tense, a number **2** for present tense, or a number **3** for future tense.

Verb Tense	Regular Verbs	Verb Tense	Irregular Verbs
	1. The band <u>will march</u> in the parade.		4. The ship <u>sinks</u> quickly.
	2. The band <u>marched</u> in the parade.		5. The ship <u>will sink</u> quickly.
	3. The band <u>marches</u> in the parade.		6. The ship <u>sank</u> quickly.

© SHURLEY INSTRUCTIONAL MATERIALS, INC.

Chapter 24, Lesson 2, Practice 2: On notebook paper, write a friendly letter to a friend or relative. Use References 27 and 28 as a guide to make sure your letter is in the correct friendly-letter format. Have your parents help you address an envelope. Mail your letter and wait for a response.

Chapter 24, Lesson 3, Practice 1: Identify the tense of each underlined verb by writing a number **1** for past tense, a number **2** for present tense, or a number **3** for future tense.

Verb Tense	Regular Verbs	Verb Tense	Irregular Verbs
	1. The cookies <u>will bake</u> in the oven.		4. The choir <u>will sing</u> in the early service.
	2. The cookies <u>bake</u> in the oven.		5. The choir <u>sang</u> in the early service.
	3. The cookies <u>baked</u> in the oven.		6. The choir <u>sings</u> in the early service.

Chapter 24, Lesson 3, Practice 2: On notebook paper, write a friendly letter to a friend or relative. Use References 27 and 28 as a guide to make sure your letter is in the correct friendly-letter format. Have your parents help you address an envelope. Mail your letter and wait for a response.

Chapter 25, Lesson 1, Practice: First, think of a person who has done something nice for you or has given you a gift (even the gift of time). On notebook paper, write a thank-you note to that person. Use the information in Reference 29 or 30 as a guide. Have your parents help you address an envelope. Mail your thank-you note.

Chapter 25, Lesson 2, Practice 1: Identify the tense of each underlined verb by writing a number **1** for past tense, a number **2** for present tense, or a number **3** for future tense.

Verb Tense	Regular Verbs	Verb Tense	Irregular Verbs
	1. The road <u>will curve</u> around the lake.		4. The author <u>wrote</u> a new play.
	2. The road <u>curved</u> around the lake.		5. The author <u>writes</u> a new play.
	3. The road <u>curves</u> around the lake.		6. The author <u>will write</u> a new play.

© SHURLEY INSTRUCTIONAL MATERIALS, INC.

Chapter 25, Lesson 2, Practice 2: First, think of a person who has done something nice for you or has given you a gift (even the gift of time). On notebook paper, write a thank-you note to that person. Use the information in Reference 29 or 30 as a guide. Have your parents help you address an envelope. Mail your thank-you note.

Chapter 25, Lesson 3, Practice 1: Identify the tense of each underlined verb by writing a number **1** for past tense, a number **2** for present tense, or a number **3** for future tense.

Verb Tense	Regular Verbs	Verb Tense	Irregular Verbs
	1. Billy <u>will wash</u> the dishes.		4. The players <u>shake</u> hands.
	2. Billy <u>washed</u> the dishes.		5. The players <u>will shake</u> hands.
	3. Billy <u>washes</u> the dishes.		6. The players <u>shook</u> hands.

Chapter 25, Lesson 3, Practice 2: Think of a person who has done something nice for you or has given you a gift (even the gift of time). On notebook paper, write a thank-you note to that person. Use the information in Reference 29 or 30 as a guide. Have your parents help you address an envelope. Mail your thank-you note.

Chapter 26, Lesson 1, Practice: Put each group of words in alphabetical order. Write numbers in the blanks to show the order in each column.

Winter Words	Family Words	"S" Words	Fruit Words
_____ 1. snow	_____ 4. sister	_____ 7. ship	_____ 10. banana
_____ 2. ice	_____ 5. father	_____ 8. sun	_____ 11. apple
_____ 3. coat	_____ 6. aunt	_____ 9. seven	_____ 12. orange

Chapter 26, Lesson 2, Practice 1: Write the letters in each group below in alphabetical order.

1. g o c w _____

2. x f n k a t _____

© SHURLEY INSTRUCTIONAL MATERIALS, INC.

Chapter 26, Lesson 2, Practice 2: Put each group of words in alphabetical order. Write numbers in the blanks to show the order in each column.

Space Words	City Words	"R" Words
_____ 1. stars	_____ 3. park	_____ 5. rabbit
_____ 2. moon	_____ 4. skyscraper	_____ 6. road

Chapter 26, Lesson 2, Practice 3: Put each group of words in alphabetical order. Write numbers in the blanks to show the order in each column.

Summer Words	"T" Words	Vegetable Words
_____ 1. sunscreen	_____ 4. tank	_____ 7. corn
_____ 2. swimsuit	_____ 5. toy	_____ 8. potato
_____ 3. vacation	_____ 6. two	_____ 9. carrot

Chapter 26, Lesson 3, Practice 1: Write the letters in each group below in alphabetical order.

1. b w j m _____

2. z p a u o e _____

Chapter 26, Lesson 3, Practice 2: Put each group of words in alphabetical order. Write numbers in the blanks to show the order in each column.

State Words	Ocean Words	"O" Words
_____ 1. Alaska	_____ 3. waves	_____ 5. otter
_____ 2. Arizona	_____ 4. whale	_____ 6. old

© SHURLEY INSTRUCTIONAL MATERIALS, INC.

Chapter 26, Lesson 3, Practice 3: Put each group of words in alphabetical order. Write numbers in the blanks to show the order in each column.

Breakfast Words	"D" Words	Movie Words
_____ 1. toast	_____ 4. duck	_____ 7. popcorn
_____ 2. eggs	_____ 5. donkey	_____ 8. soda
_____ 3. milk	_____ 6. dog	_____ 9. candy

Chapter 26, Lesson 4, Practice 1: Write the letters in each group below in alphabetical order.

1. l h r c _____

2. f i k o w r _____

Chapter 26, Lesson 4, Practice 2: Put each group of words in alphabetical order. Write numbers in the blanks to show the order in each column.

Transportation Words	Tool Words	"J" Words
_____ 1. bus	_____ 3. drill	_____ 5. jet
_____ 2. boat	_____ 4. hammer	_____ 6. jelly

Chapter 26, Lesson 4, Practice 3: Put each group of words in alphabetical order. Write numbers in the blanks to show the order in each column.

Hospital Words	"D" Words	Clothing Words
_____ 1. nurse	_____ 4. deer	_____ 7. shirt
_____ 2. patient	_____ 5. duck	_____ 8. skirt
_____ 3. doctor	_____ 6. dog	_____ 9. sweater

© SHURLEY INSTRUCTIONAL MATERIALS, INC.

Chapter 27, Lesson 3, Practice 1: Underline the correct answer in each sentence.

1. Nonfiction books contain information and stories that are (**true, not true**).
2. Fiction books contain information and stories that are (**true, not true**).
3. The most common reference books are the dictionary and the encyclopedia. (**true, not true**)

Chapter 27, Lesson 3, Practice 2: Put each group of words in alphabetical order. Write numbers in the blanks to show the order in each column.

Adjective Words	**"G" Words**	**Cleaning Words**
_____ 1. squirmy	_____ 4. grasshopper	_____ 7. rags
_____ 2. strong	_____ 5. goats	_____ 8. broom
_____ 3. silly	_____ 6. giant	_____ 9. mop

Chapter 27, Lesson 4, Practice 1: Underline the correct answer in each sentence.

1. Nonfiction books contain information and stories that are (**true, not true**).
2. Fiction books contain information and stories that are (**true, not true**).
3. The most common reference books are the dictionary and the encyclopedia. (**true, not true**)

Chapter 27, Lesson 4, Practice 2: Put each group of words in alphabetical order. Write numbers in the blanks to show the order in each column.

Preposition Words	**Verb Words**	**Pet Words**
_____ 1. in	_____ 4. erupted	_____ 7. pony
_____ 2. to	_____ 5. camped	_____ 8. cat
_____ 3. on	_____ 6. yawned	_____ 9. dog

© SHURLEY INSTRUCTIONAL MATERIALS, INC.

TEST

SECTION

Chapter 7 Test

Exercise 1: Classify each sentence. Use **SN** for subject noun, **V** for verb, and **Adv** for adverb.

1. Cats jumped quickly.

2. Puppies played quietly yesterday.

Exercise 2: Underline the **syn** if the words are synonyms. Underline the **ant** if the words are antonyms.

1. in, out	**syn ant**	2. quit, stop	**syn ant**	3. right, wrong	**syn ant**

Exercise 3: In your journal, write a paragraph summarizing what you have learned this week.

© SHURLEY INSTRUCTIONAL MATERIALS, INC.

Chapter 8 Test

Exercise 1: Classify each sentence. Use **SN** for subject noun, **V** for verb, **Adv** for adverb, and **Adj** for adjective.

1. Three squirmy puppies barked loudly today.

2. Two brown ducks sat quietly yesterday.

Exercise 2: Underline the **syn** if the words are synonyms. Underline the **ant** if the words are antonyms.

1. stone, rock	**syn ant**	2. warm, cold	**syn ant**	3. over, under	**syn ant**

Exercise 3: In your journal, write a paragraph summarizing what you have learned this week.

© SHURLEY INSTRUCTIONAL MATERIALS, INC.

Chapter 9 Test

Exercise 1: Classify each sentence. Use **SN** for subject noun, **V** for verb, **Adv** for adverb, **Adj** for adjective, and **A** for article adjective.

1. The three yellow cats walked quietly today.

2. A brown horse raced quickly away.

Exercise 2: Underline the **syn** if the words are synonyms. Underline the **ant** if the words are antonyms.

1. start, begin	**syn ant**	2. up, down	**syn ant**	3. push, pull	**syn ant**

Exercise 3: Name the four parts of speech that you have studied. (*You may use abbreviations.*)

1._____ 2._____ 3._____ 4. _____

Exercise 4: In your journal, write a paragraph summarizing what you have learned this week.

© SHURLEY INSTRUCTIONAL MATERIALS, INC.

Chapter 10 Test

Exercise 1: Classify each sentence. Use **SN** for subject noun, **V** for verb, **Adv** for adverb, **Adj** for adjective, and **A** for article adjective. For Sentence 1, underline the complete subject one time and the complete predicate two times.

1. The five big ships sailed home yesterday.

2. An excited dog barked loudly today.

Exercise 2: Underline the **syn** if the words are synonyms. Underline the **ant** if the words are antonyms.

1. front, back	**syn ant**	2. rough, smooth	**syn ant**	3. giant, huge	**syn ant**

Exercise 3: Name the four parts of speech that you have studied. (*You may use abbreviations.*)

1._____ 2._____ 3._____ 4. _____

Exercise 4: In your journal, write a paragraph summarizing what you have learned this week.

© SHURLEY INSTRUCTIONAL MATERIALS, INC.

Chapter 11 Test

Exercise 1: Classify each sentence. Use **SN** for subject noun, **V** for verb, **Adv** for adverb, **Adj** for adjective, and **A** for article adjective. For Sentence 2, underline the complete subject one time and the complete predicate two times

1. The three silly clowns ran around happily.

2. A beautiful black car stopped suddenly.

Exercise 2: Underline the **syn** if the words are synonyms. Underline the **ant** if the words are antonyms.

1. inside, outside	**syn ant**	2. form, shape	**syn ant**	3. end, finish	**syn ant**

Exercise 3: Name the four parts of speech that you have studied. (*You may use abbreviations.*)

1._____ 2._____ 3._____ 4. _____

Exercise 4: On notebook paper, write each sentence correctly. Capitalize the first word of each sentence and put a (**.**) or a (**?**) at the end.

1. the yellow cab stopped suddenly
2. did the home team win yesterday

Exercise 5: On notebook paper, write a sentence using the words in the Word Bank. Put the words you select in the same order as the Sentence Labels listed below. Write the correct label above each word in your sentence.

WORD BANK			
Nouns	**Verbs**	**Adjectives**	**Adverbs**
bird ant snake	scurried, climbed, crawled, flew, ate, slithered, hopped	a, an, the, two, busy, tiny, hungry, huge, green, pretty, yellow, black, funny, little, excited	hastily, slowly, quickly, suddenly, fast, today, silently, around, early, away
Sentence Labels: A Adj SN V Adv (Bonus) A Adj Adj SN V Adv Adv			

Exercise 6: In your journal, write a paragraph summarizing what you have learned this week.

© SHURLEY INSTRUCTIONAL MATERIALS, INC.

Chapter 12 Test

Exercise 1: Classify each sentence. Use **SN** for subject noun, **V** for verb, **Adv** for adverb, **Adj** for adjective, and **A** for article adjective. For Sentence 2, underline the complete subject one time and the complete predicate two times

1. The red flowers grew rapidly.

2. Six large jets flew fast today.

Exercise 2: Underline the **syn** if the words are synonyms. Underline the **ant** if the words are antonyms.

1. open, close	**syn ant**	2. tiny, small	**syn ant**	3. high, low	**syn ant**

Exercise 3: Name the four parts of speech that you have studied. (*You may use abbreviations.*)

1._____ 2._____ 3._____ 4. _____

Exercise 4: Write ***a*** or ***an*** in the blanks.

1. The cat chased _____ ant.
2. We made _____ cake.
3. Pat carved _____ pumpkin.
4. The house has _____ door.
5. ____ arm
6. ____ mat
7. ____ insect
8. ____ elevator

Exercise 5: On notebook paper, write a sentence using the words in the Word Bank. Put the words you select in the same order as the Sentence Labels listed below. Write the correct label above each word in your sentence.

WORD BANK			
Nouns	**Verbs**	**Adjectives**	**Adverbs**
men women students	walked, laughed, ran, talked, fished, looked, shouted, stopped, worked, yawned, drove	a, an, the, several, young, friendly, big, happy, cheerful, busy, weary, tired, frightened, eager, excited	easily, happily, quietly, slowly, suddenly, today, rapidly, away, carefully, early, loudly
Sentence Labels: A Adj SN V Adv		**(Bonus) A Adj Adj SN V Adv Adv**	

Exercise 6: In your journal, write a paragraph summarizing what you have learned this week.

© SHURLEY INSTRUCTIONAL MATERIALS, INC.

Chapter 13 Test

Exercise 1: Classify each sentence. Use **SN** for subject noun, **V** for verb, **Adv** for adverb, **Adj** for adjective, **A** for article adjective, **P** for preposition, and **OP** for object of the preposition. For Sentence 1, underline the complete subject one time and the complete predicate two times.

1. The busy little bee landed softly on the flower.

2. The poor girl fell in the mud.

Exercise 2: Underline the **syn** if the words are synonyms. Underline the **ant** if the words are antonyms.

1. part, piece	**syn ant**	2. far, near	**syn ant**	3. rush, hurry	**syn ant**

Exercise 3: Name the five parts of speech that you have studied. (*You may use abbreviations.*)

1._____ 2. _____ 3. _____ 4. _____ 5. _____

Exercise 4: Write ***a*** or ***an*** in the blanks.

1. He was stranded on ____ island.
2. I saw ____ deer in the woods.
3. Pat planted ____ garden.
4. The birds built ____ nest.
5. ____ odor
6. ____ jar
7. ____ eel
8. ____ album

Exercise 5: In your journal, write a paragraph summarizing what you have learned this week.

© SHURLEY INSTRUCTIONAL MATERIALS, INC.

Chapter 14 Test

Exercise 1: Classify each sentence. Use **SN** for subject noun, **V** for verb, **Adv** for adverb, **Adj** for adjective, **A** for article adjective, **P** for preposition, and **OP** for object of the preposition. For Sentence 1, underline the complete subject one time and the complete predicate two times.

1. The beautiful music played softly in the store.

2. A frightened brown duck flew across the road today.

Exercise 2: Underline the **syn** if the words are synonyms. Underline the **ant** if the words are antonyms.

1. old, new	**syn ant**	2. lean, thin	**syn ant**	3. above, below	**syn ant**

Exercise 3: Name the five parts of speech that you have studied. (*You may use abbreviations.*)

1._____ 2. _____ 3. _____ 4. _____ 5. _____

Exercise 4: Write ***a*** or ***an*** in the blanks.

1. Jan boiled _____ egg.
2. He works in _____ factory.
3. The actor wore _____ mask.
4. Lisa ate _____ apple.
5. ____ officer
6. ____ fire
7. ____ eye
8. ____ napkin

Exercise 5: On notebook paper, write a sentence using the words in the Word Bank. Put the words you select in the same order as the Sentence Labels listed below. Write the correct label above each word in your sentence.

WORD BANK

Nouns	Verbs	Adjectives	Adverbs	Prepositional Phrases
teacher coaches friend	waved smiled talked	a, an, the, friendly, busy, new, eager, several, enthusiastic	warmly, patiently, happily, today	at the children to the parents to the players

Sentence Labels: A Adj Adj SN V Adv Prep Phrase

Exercise 6: In your journal, write a paragraph summarizing what you have learned this week.

© SHURLEY INSTRUCTIONAL MATERIALS, INC.

Chapter 15 Test

Exercise 1: Classify each sentence. Use **SN** for subject noun, **V** for verb, **Adv** for adverb, **Adj** for adjective, **A** for article adjective, **P** for preposition, and **OP** for object of the preposition. For Sentence 1, underline the complete subject one time and the complete predicate two times.

1. The eight shivering puppies whimpered loudly.

2. The big ocean waves crashed loudly across the rocks.

Exercise 2: Underline the **syn** if the words are synonyms. Underline the **ant** if the words are antonyms.

1. left, right	**syn ant**	2. poor, rich	**syn ant**	3. puzzle, riddle	**syn ant**

Exercise 3: Name the five parts of speech that you have studied. (*You may use abbreviations.*)

1._____ 2. _____ 3. _____ 4. _____ 5. _____

Exercise 4: Correct the capitalization mistakes and put the rule number above each correction. Use the rule numbers in Reference 11 on page 17 in the Reference Section of your book. Put a (.) or a (?) at the end of the sentence.

_____**(capitalization rule numbers)**

i will ride to school with katie on tuesday ____ **(3 capitals)**

Exercise 5: On notebook paper, write a sentence using the words in the Word Bank. Put the words you select in the same order as the Sentence Labels listed below. Write the correct label above each word in your sentence.

WORD BANK

Nouns	Verbs	Adjectives	Adverbs	Prepositional Phrases
fox squirrel raccoon	peeked stared glanced	a, an, the, baby, cute, tiny, tired, red, large, frisky, curious, hungry, playful	suddenly excitedly cautiously curiously	in the box at the boy at the house across the yard

Sentence Labels: A Adj Adj SN V Adv Prep Phrase

Exercise 6: In your journal, write a paragraph summarizing what you have learned this week.

© SHURLEY INSTRUCTIONAL MATERIALS, INC.

Chapter 16 Test

Exercise 1: Classify each sentence. Use **SN** for subject noun, **V** for verb, **Adv** for adverb, **Adj** for adjective, **A** for article adjective, **P** for preposition, and **OP** for object of the preposition. For Sentence 1, underline the complete subject one time and the complete predicate two times.

1. Nine yellow kites flew silently across the lake.

2. The huge rocks rolled suddenly down the mountain.

Exercise 2: Underline the **syn** if the words are synonyms. Underline the **ant** if the words are antonyms.

1. on, off	**syn ant**	2. tall, short	**syn ant**	3. kind, good	**syn ant**

Exercise 3: Name the five parts of speech that you have studied. (*You may use abbreviations.*)

1._____ 2. _____ 3. _____ 4. _____ 5. _____

Exercise 4: Correct the capitalization mistakes and put the rule number above each correction. Use the rule numbers in Reference 11 on page 17 in the Reference Section of your book. Put a (.) or a (?) at the end of the sentence.

_____**(capitalization rule numbers)**

does walter live in miami, florida _____ **(4 capitals)**

Exercise 5: For each noun listed below, write **S** for singular or **P** for plural.

Noun	S or P	Noun	S or P	Noun	S or P
1. bats		5. boys		9. parrot	
2. woman		6. lady		10. children	
3. nests		7. women		11. piano	
4. apple		8. child		12. telephones	

Exercise 6: In your journal, write a paragraph summarizing what you have learned this week.

© SHURLEY INSTRUCTIONAL MATERIALS, INC.

Chapter 17 Test

Exercise 1: Classify each sentence. Use **SN** for subject noun, **V** for verb, **Adv** for adverb, **Adj** for adjective, **A** for article adjective, **P** for preposition, and **OP** for object of the preposition. For Sentence 2, underline the complete subject one time and the complete predicate two times.

1. The big volcano erupted suddenly yesterday.

2. Several dogs barked loudly at the car.

Exercise 2: Underline the **syn** if the words are synonyms. Underline the **ant** if the words are antonyms.

1. top, bottom	**syn ant**	2. evil, bad	**syn ant**	3. hard, firm	**syn ant**

Exercise 3: Name the five parts of speech that you have studied. (*You may use abbreviations.*)

1._____ 2. _____ 3. _____ 4. _____ 5. _____

Exercise 4: Correct the capitalization mistakes and put the rule number above each correction. Use the rule numbers in Reference 11 on page 17 in the Reference Section of your book. Put a (.) or a (?) at the end of the sentence.

_____**(capitalization rule numbers)**

i would like to visit alex in march ____ **(3 capitals)**

Exercise 5: Write **S** for singular or **P** for plural.

Noun	S or P
1. jar	
2. notebooks	
3. computer	
4. mice	

Exercise 6: Write **C** for Common or **P** for proper.

Noun	C or P
1. Mississippi	
2. James	
3. nephew	
4. window	

Exercise 7: In your journal, write a paragraph summarizing what you have learned this week.

© SHURLEY INSTRUCTIONAL MATERIALS, INC.

Chapter 18 Test

Exercise 1: Classify each sentence. Use **SN** for subject noun, **V** for verb, **Adv** for adverb, **Adj** for adjective, **A** for article adjective, **P** for preposition, and **OP** for object of the preposition. For Sentence 1, underline the complete subject one time and the complete predicate two times.

1. The excited children played in the snow today.

2. Pink flowers grew by the gate.

Exercise 2: Underline the **syn** if the words are synonyms. Underline the **ant** if the words are antonyms.

1. sick, ill	**syn ant**	2. before, after	**syn ant**	3. lost, found	**syn ant**

Exercise 3: Name the five parts of speech that you have studied. (*You may use abbreviations.*)

1._____ 2._____ 3._____ 4._____ 5._____

Exercise 4: Write the name of the topic that best describes what each column of words is about. Choose from these topics: **Colors** **Family** **Animals** **Bathroom Things** **Food**

(1)	**(2)**	**(3)**
_____	_____	_____
bread	uncle	shower
meat	cousin	shampoo
pasta	sister	towel

Exercise 5: In each column, cross out the one idea that does not support the underlined topic at the top.

(1)	(2)	(3)
Months	**Desserts**	**Days**
July	pie	Saturday
jail	cake	Wednesday
January	cookie	France
June	playground	Thursday

Exercise 6: Read each topic. Then, cross out the one sentence that does not support the topic.

A. Topic: My Favorite Color

1. My favorite color is yellow.
2. Yellow reminds me of sunshine.
3. I painted my room yellow.
4. Red and blue make purple.

B. Topic: In the City

1. I take a taxi to work every day in the city.
2. My apartment in the city is on the fifth floor.
3. I grew up in the country.
4. I have lived in the city for three years.

Exercise 7: In your journal, write a paragraph summarizing what you have learned this week.

© SHURLEY INSTRUCTIONAL MATERIALS, INC.

Chapter 19 Test

Exercise 1: Classify each sentence. Use **SN** for subject noun, **V** for verb, **Adv** for adverb, **Adj** for adjective, **A** for article adjective, **P** for preposition, and **OP** for object of the preposition. For Sentence 1, underline the complete subject one time and the complete predicate two times.

1. The kind nurse talked quietly to the patient.

2. The three busy brothers worked hard.

Exercise 2: Underline the **syn** if the words are synonyms. Underline the **ant** if the words are antonyms.

1. front, back	**syn ant**	2. simple, easy	**syn ant**	3. early, late	**syn ant**

Exercise 3: Name the five parts of speech that you have studied. (*You may use abbreviations.*)

1._____ 2. _____ 3. _____ 4. _____ 5. _____

Exercise 4: Correct the capitalization mistakes and put the rule number above each correction. Use the rule numbers in Reference 11 on page 17 in the Reference Section of your book. Put a (.) or a (?) at the end of the sentence.

_____**(capitalization rule numbers)**

does bob work at a factory in jefferson city, missouri ____ **(5 capitals)**

Exercise 5: Write the name of the topic that best describes what each column of words is about. Choose from these topics: **Colors** **Clothing** **Animals** **Kitchen Things** **Plants**

(1)	**(2)**	**(3)**
_____	_____	_____
deer	sweater	tree
swan	shorts	grass
bear	shirts	flowers

Exercise 6: In each column, cross out the one idea that does not support the underlined topic at the top.

(1)	(2)	(3)
School Supplies	**Winter Weather**	**People**
paper	snow	customer
turkey	sleet	teenager
pencil	ice	pickle
ruler	chicken	sister

Exercise 7: In your journal, write a paragraph summarizing what you have learned this week.

© SHURLEY INSTRUCTIONAL MATERIALS, INC.

Chapter 20 Test

Exercise 1: Classify each sentence. Use **SN** for subject noun, **V** for verb, **Adv** for adverb, **Adj** for adjective, **A** for article adjective, **P** for preposition, and **OP** for object of the preposition. For Sentence 2, underline the complete subject one time and the complete predicate two times.

1. The three friends raced excitedly to the boat.

2. The cute little fireflies glowed brightly in the dark.

Exercise 2: Underline the **syn** if the words are synonyms. Underline the **ant** if the words are antonyms.

1. slow, quick	**syn ant**	2. first, last	**syn ant**	3. raise, lift	**syn ant**

Exercise 3: Name the five parts of speech that you have studied. (*You may use abbreviations.*)

1._____ 2._____ 3._____ 4._____ 5._____

Exercise 4: Correct the capitalization mistakes and put the rule number above each correction. Use the rule numbers in Reference 11 on page 17 in the Reference Section of your book. Put a (**.**) or a (**?**) at the end of the sentence.

_____**(capitalization rule numbers)**

our company meets in tulsa on the second friday in july ____ **(4 capitals)**

Exercise 5: Write the name of the topic that best describes what each column of words is about. Choose from these topics: **Colors** **People** **Ocean Animals** **Shapes** **Sports**.

(1)	**(2)**	**(3)**
_____	_____	_____
whale	baseball	pilot
shrimp	football	niece
shark	tennis	pastor

Exercise 6: In each column, cross out the one idea that does not support the underlined topic.

(1)	(2)	(3)
Vegetables	**Months**	**Insects**
beans	December	wasp
finger	April	mosquito
corn	October	butter
potato	Jacob	ant

Exercise 7: In your journal, write a paragraph summarizing what you have learned this week.

© SHURLEY INSTRUCTIONAL MATERIALS, INC.

Chapter 21 Test

Exercise 1: Classify each sentence. Use **SN** for subject noun, **V** for verb, **Adv** for adverb, **Adj** for adjective, **A** for article adjective, **P** for preposition, and **OP** for object of the preposition. For Sentence 2, underline the complete subject one time and the complete predicate two times.

1. The beautiful butterfly flew quickly away.

2. The fireman climbed carefully to the roof.

Exercise 2: Underline the **syn** if the words are synonyms. Underline the **ant** if the words are antonyms.

1. below, beneath	**syn ant**	2. sweet, sour	**syn ant**	3. aid, help	**syn ant**

Exercise 3: Name the five parts of speech that you have studied. (*You may use abbreviations.*)

1._____ 2. _____ 3. _____ 4. _____ 5. _____

Exercise 4: Match each subject part with the correct predicate part by writing the correct sentence number in the blank.

1. The player _____ climbed in the trees.
2. The fire _____ hatched today.
3. The tiny egg _____ threw the ball.
4. Three monkeys _____ baked in the oven.
5. An apple pie _____ burned brightly.

Exercise 5: Write **S** for a complete sentence and **F** for a sentence fragment on the line beside each group of words below.

_____ 1. The ants marched across the ground.
_____ 2. To the man in the car.
_____ 3. Many workers ride the subway.
_____ 4. That new building.
_____ 5. Walter made several friends on the bus.
_____ 6. The pain in his right hand.
_____ 7. Paid for the ticket with cash.
_____ 8. At the bottom of the closet.
_____ 9. Telephone rang.

Exercise 6: In your journal, write a paragraph summarizing what you have learned this week.

© SHURLEY INSTRUCTIONAL MATERIALS, INC.

Chapter 22 Test

Exercise 1: Classify each sentence. Use **SN** for subject noun, **V** for verb, **Adv** for adverb, **Adj** for adjective, **A** for article adjective, **P** for preposition, and **OP** for object of the preposition. For Sentence 1, underline the complete subject one time and the complete predicate two times.

1. The pretty birthday candles melted slowly on the cake.

2. The excited children ran to the pool.

Exercise 2: Underline the **syn** if the words are synonyms. Underline the **ant** if the words are antonyms.

1. night, day	**syn ant**	2. bashful, shy	**syn ant**	3. shout, whisper	**syn ant**

Exercise 3: Name the five parts of speech that you have studied. (*You may use abbreviations.*)

1._____ 2. _____ 3. _____ 4. _____ 5. _____

Exercise 4: Correct the capitalization mistakes and put the rule number above each correction. Use the rule numbers in Reference 11 on page 17 in the Reference Section of your book. Put a (.) or a (?) at the end of the sentence.

_____**(capitalization rule numbers)**

our church meets every sunday night in september ___ **(3 capitals)**

Exercise 5: Write the correct contraction in each blank. Use the contraction references to help you.

1. do not _____
2. cannot _____
3. I am _____
4. are not _____
5. were not _____

Exercise 6: Write the correct words beside each contraction. Use the contraction references to help you.

1. didn't _____
2. wasn't _____
3. doesn't _____
4. isn't _____
5. I'm _____

Exercise 7: In your journal, write a paragraph summarizing what you have learned this week.

© SHURLEY INSTRUCTIONAL MATERIALS, INC.

Chapter 23 Test

Exercise 1: Classify each sentence. Use **SN** for subject noun, **V** for verb, **Adv** for adverb, **Adj** for adjective, **A** for article adjective, **P** for preposition, and **OP** for object of the preposition. For Sentence 2, underline the complete subject one time and the complete predicate two times.

1. The family ate cheerfully in the kitchen tonight.

2. Tim drove quickly to school.

Exercise 2: Underline the **syn** if the words are synonyms. Underline the **ant** if the words are antonyms.

1. calm, quiet	**syn ant**	2. ask, tell	**syn ant**	3. sell, buy	**syn ant**

Exercise 3: Name the five parts of speech that you have studied. (*You may use abbreviations.*)

1._____ 2. _____ 3. _____ 4. _____ 5. _____

Exercise 4: Identify the tense of each underlined verb by writing a number **1** for past tense, a number **2** for present tense, or a number **3** for future tense.

Verb Tense	Regular Verbs	Verb Tense	Irregular Verbs
	1. The girls skipped down the street.		7. Mom gives me a big hug.
	2. The girls will skip down the street.		8. Mom will give me a big hug.
	3. The girls skip down the street.		9. Mom gave me a big hug.
	4. Janet works at the bank.		10. The wind blew against the window.
	5. Janet will work at the bank.		11. The wind will blow against the window.
	6. Janet worked at the bank.		12. The wind blows against the window.

Exercise 5: Write the correct contraction in each blank. Use the contraction references to help you.

1. do not _____
2. cannot _____
3. I am _____
4. are not _____
5. were not _____

Exercise 6: Write the correct words beside each contraction. Use the contraction references to help you.

1. didn't _____
2. wasn't _____
3. doesn't _____
4. isn't _____
5. I'm _____

Exercise 7: In your journal, write a paragraph summarizing what you have learned this week.

© SHURLEY INSTRUCTIONAL MATERIALS, INC.

Chapter 24 Test

Exercise 1: Classify each sentence. Use **SN** for subject noun, **V** for verb, **Adv** for adverb, **Adj** for adjective, **A** for article adjective, **P** for preposition, and **OP** for object of the preposition. For Sentence 2, underline the complete subject one time and the complete predicate two times.

1. The bouncy little puppies barked loudly in the store.

2. Grandmother laughed at the grandchildren.

Exercise 2: Underline the **syn** if the words are synonyms. Underline the **ant** if the words are antonyms.

1. wild, tame	**syn ant**	2. push, shove	**syn ant**	3. add, subtract	**syn ant**

Exercise 3: Name the five parts of speech that you have studied. (*You may use abbreviations.*)

1._____ 2. _____ 3. _____ 4. _____ 5. _____

Exercise 4: Identify the tense of each underlined verb by writing a number **1** for past tense, a number **2** for present tense, or a number **3** for future tense.

Verb Tense	Regular Verbs	Verb Tense	Irregular Verbs
	1. The cars will race around the track.		4. My flowers grow in the spring.
	2. The cars raced around the track.		5. My flowers will grow in the spring.
	3. The cars race around the track.		6. My flowers grew in the spring.

Exercise 5: Write the correct contraction in each blank. Use the contraction references to help you.

1. do not _____
2. cannot _____
3. I am _____
4. are not _____
5. were not _____

Exercise 6: Write the correct words beside each contraction. Use the contraction references to help you.

1. didn't _____
2. wasn't _____
3. doesn't _____
4. isn't _____
5. I'm _____

Exercise 7: On notebook paper, write a friendly letter to a friend or relative. Use References 27 and 28 as a guide to make sure your letter is in the correct friendly-letter format. Have your parents help you address an envelope. Mail your letter and wait for a response.

Exercise 8: In your journal, write a paragraph summarizing what you have learned this week.

© SHURLEY INSTRUCTIONAL MATERIALS, INC.

Chapter 25 Test

Exercise 1: Classify each sentence. Use **SN** for subject noun, **V** for verb, **Adv** for adverb, **Adj** for adjective, **A** for article adjective, **P** for preposition, and **OP** for object of the preposition. For Sentence 1, underline the complete subject one time and the complete predicate two times.

1. The tiny beetle crawled carefully across the rocks.

2. The white snow melted quickly.

Exercise 2: Underline the **syn** if the words are synonyms. Underline the **ant** if the words are antonyms.

1. round, square	**syn ant**	2. pull, tug	**syn ant**	3. bright, dim	**syn ant**

Exercise 3: Name the five parts of speech that you have studied. (*You may use abbreviations.*)

1._____ 2. _____ 3. _____ 4. _____ 5. _____

Exercise 4: Write the correct contraction in each blank. Use the contraction references to help you.

1. do not _____
2. cannot _____
3. I am _____
4. are not _____
5. were not _____

Exercise 5: Write the correct words beside each contraction. Use the contraction references to help you.

1. didn't _____
2. wasn't _____
3. doesn't _____
4. isn't _____
5. I'm _____

Exercise 6: First, think of a person who has done something nice for you or has given you a *gift (even the gift of time)*. On notebook paper, write a thank-you note to that person. Use the information in Reference 29 or 30 as a guide. Have your parents help you address an envelope. Mail your thank-you note.

Exercise 7: In your journal, write a paragraph summarizing what you have learned this week.

© SHURLEY INSTRUCTIONAL MATERIALS, INC.

Chapter 26 Test

Exercise 1: Classify each sentence. Use **SN** for subject noun, **V** for verb, **Adv** for adverb, **Adj** for adjective, **A** for article adjective, **P** for preposition, and **OP** for object of the preposition. For Sentence 1, underline the complete subject one time and the complete predicate two times.

1. The cute little rabbits hopped quickly away.

2. Several young children played happily in the park.

Exercise 2: Write the letters in each group below in alphabetical order.

1. k d r n _____

2. h a s m o u _____

Exercise 3: Put each group of words in alphabetical order. Use numbers to show the order in each column.

Zoo Words	Color Words	"B" Words
_____ 1. giraffe	_____ 5. yellow	_____ 9. brothers
_____ 2. monkey	_____ 6. green	_____ 10. buzzed
_____ 3. elephant	_____ 7. pink	_____ 11. beavers
_____ 4. tiger	_____ 8. red	_____ 12. balloon

Exercise 4: Put each group of words in alphabetical order. Use numbers to show the order in each column.

Food Words	"C" Words	Tree Words
_____ 1. taco	_____ 6. clowns	_____ 11. oak
_____ 2. hamburger	_____ 7. crib	_____ 12. maple
_____ 3. pizza	_____ 8. cute	_____ 13. walnut
_____ 4. hotdogs	_____ 9. church	_____ 14. cedar
_____ 5. steak	_____ 10. cats	_____ 15. pine

Exercise 5: In your journal, write a paragraph summarizing what you have learned this week.

© SHURLEY INSTRUCTIONAL MATERIALS, INC.

Chapter 27 Test

Exercise 1: Classify each sentence. Use **SN** for subject noun, **V** for verb, **Adv** for adverb, **Adj** for adjective, **A** for article adjective, **P** for preposition, and **OP** for object of the preposition. For Sentence 1, underline the complete subject one time and the complete predicate two times.

1. The funny frog hopped in the water.

2. The three pretty lamps burned brightly today.

Exercise 2: Name the five parts of speech that you have studied. (*You may use abbreviations.*)

1._____ 2. _____ 3. _____ 4. _____ 5. _____

Exercise 3: Write the correct contraction in each blank. Use the contraction references to help you.

1. do not _____
2. cannot _____
3. I am _____
4. are not _____
5. were not _____

Exercise 4: Write the correct words beside each contraction. Use the contraction references to help you.

1. didn't _____
2. wasn't _____
3. doesn't _____
4. isn't _____
5. I'm _____

Exercise 5: Underline the correct answer in each sentence.

1. Fiction books contain information and stories that are (**true, not true**).
2. Nonfiction books contain information and stories that are (**true, not true**).
3. The most common reference books are the dictionary and the encyclopedia. (**true, not true**)

Exercise 6: Put each group of words in alphabetical order. Use numbers to show the order in each column.

Number Words	Adverb Words	Proper Noun Words
_____ 1. two	_____ 5. carefully	_____ 9. Dan
_____ 2. three	_____ 6. away	_____ 10. Anna
_____ 3. four	_____ 7. today	_____ 11. Tim
_____ 4. five	_____ 8. suddenly	_____ 12. Sam

Exercise 7: In your journal, write a paragraph summarizing what you have learned this week.

© SHURLEY INSTRUCTIONAL MATERIALS, INC.

ACTIVITY

SECTION

ACTIVITY / ASSIGNMENT TIME

Chapter 1, Lesson 4, Activity: Use one sheet of brown construction paper, one sheet of white construction paper, and one sheet of blue construction paper. Follow the directions given below to create different transportation groups.

1. On the brown sheet of paper, draw pictures of roads, trees, and flowers. Then, using newspapers, magazines, catalogs, etc., cut and paste several examples of ground transportation. (Examples: cars, trucks, vans, bicycles, motorcycles)

2. On the white sheet of paper, draw a sun, clouds, and birds. Then, cut and paste several examples of air transportation. (Examples: airplanes, helicopters, blimps, hot-air balloons)

3. On the blue sheet of paper, draw ocean waves and fish. Then, cut and paste several examples of water transportation. (Examples: motor boats, sail boats, cruise ships, jet skis, barges, submarines)

Chapter 2, Lesson 2, Activity: In the Word Search Puzzle below, find the following words and color each one a different color. The words will appear "down" or "across" in the puzzle.

ANIMALS ***PEOPLE*** ***PLACES*** ***TOYS***

T	P	L	A	C	E	S
P	Q	A	U	S	K	B
E	W	N	I	D	L	N
O	E	I	O	F	Z	T
P	R	M	P	G	X	O
L	T	A	A	H	C	Y
E	Y	L	B	O	Y	S
S	D	S	F	P	L	E

© SHURLEY INSTRUCTIONAL MATERIALS, INC.

Chapter 2, Lesson 4, Activity: Choose four pieces of different-colored construction paper. Follow the directions given below to create different animal groups.

1. On the first piece of paper, write the title **Farm Animals**.
2. On the second piece of paper, write the title **Animal Pets**.
3. On the third piece of paper, write the title **Zoo Animals**.
4. On the fourth piece of paper, write the title **Jungle Animals**.
5. Search through old magazines, catalogs, newspapers, and books for examples of animals that would fit under each animal title.
6. Cut out and paste pictures of the animals on the appropriate pieces of construction paper. You may want to draw a few animals of your own.

Chapter 3, Lesson 4, Activity 2: In the Word Search Puzzle below, find the following words and color each one a different color. The words will appear "down" or "across" in the puzzle.

HEAR ***SIGHT*** ***SMELL*** ***TASTE*** ***TOUCH***

S	M	E	L	L	A	S
U	E	Q	I	E	E	T
S	L	T	G	H	H	O
I	L	A	H	E	M	U
G	T	S	C	A	B	C
H	O	T	K	R	G	H
T	W	E	S	T	E	K

Chapter 4, Lesson 5, Activity: Write the correct numbers in the blanks to match the seasons with their activities. On writing paper, write a story about one of the seasons below.

_____Spring

_____Winter

_____Autumn

_____Summer

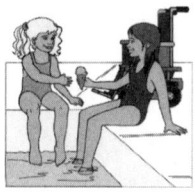

1

2

3

4

© SHURLEY INSTRUCTIONAL MATERIALS, INC.

Chapter 5, Lesson 5, Activity 2: Help sing the Noun Soup Chant listed below.

Mmmm, hot, delicious noun soup. I am making noun soup. I need nouns for my soup. Won't you add a noun to my soup? This is hot, delicious noun soup. Please add a noun to my soup. Ahhh, yummy, yummy noun soup. It makes the tummy, tummy glad for noun soup. Mmmm, hot, delicious noun soup.

Thank you for helping with my noun soup. We are having fun making hot, delicious noun soup. Look at the nouns, swirling around, in our noun soup! Ahhh, noun soup, hot delicious noun soup.

Chapter 6, Lesson 3, Activity: Find all the nouns in the boxes below. Then, color each noun box yellow.

girls	**ran**	**cats**
sat	**bears**	**walked**
boys	**played**	**dogs**

Chapter 6, Lesson 4, Activity: Find all the verbs in the boxes below. Then, color each verb box red.

walked	**played**	**cats**
girls	**ran**	**sat**
boys	**airplane**	**flew**

Chapter 7, Lesson 3, Activity: Find all the synonyms words in the boxes below and color them orange. Then, find the antonym words and color them green.

sit, stand	**lost, found**	**leap, jump**
boat, ship	**start, begin**	**empty, full**
easy, hard	**small, little**	**sad, happy**

© SHURLEY INSTRUCTIONAL MATERIALS, INC.

Chapter 7, Lesson 5, Activity: In the Word Search Puzzle below, find the following words and color each one a different color. The words will appear "down" or "across" in the puzzle.

ADVERB ***ANTONYM*** ***NOUN*** ***SYNONYM*** ***VERB***

S	Y	N	O	N	Y	M
A	V	S	A	C	Q	W
A	N	T	O	N	Y	M
N	T	H	K	O	P	N
R	V	E	R	B	S	O
F	G	H	J	L	K	U
A	D	V	E	R	B	N

Chapter 9, Lesson 3, Activity: Follow the directions below to make a noun box.

Cover a shoe box and the lid of the shoe box with white paper. You can use glue or tape to make the white paper fit the box neatly. This is your noun box. Divide the inside of the shoe box into three sections with two cardboard pieces. Identify each section as **person, place,** or **thing**. Using items around the house *(magazines, catalogs, books, travel brochures, etc.),* cut out pictures of nouns and place them in their appropriate section.

Each night, have a member of the family draw a noun from the box. The family member must use the noun in a sentence that he/she writes on a strip of paper. After you read their sentence, color the sentence strip and glue it on the noun box. Friends and other relatives may also participate in decorating the noun box with sentence strips. They should sign their names on the sentence strips they have written. Later, another game can be played to guess who wrote the sentences using the nouns from the noun box. Everyone can guess who wrote the most sentences.

Chapter 10, Lesson 4, Activity: Use the code in the box below to find grammar words. Using the code numbers, write the correct letters for each blank. Then, make up your own code for several words.

Code		**Words**	
1. n	7. j		
2. d	8. r	___ ___ ___ ___	___ ___ ___ ___ ___ ___
3. a	9. e	1 6 5 1	3 2 4 9 8 10
4. v	10. b		
5. u	11. t	___ ___ ___ ___	___ ___ ___ ___ ___ ___ ___ ___ ___
6. o	12. i	4 9 8 10	3 2 7 9 13 11 12 4 9
	13. c		

© SHURLEY INSTRUCTIONAL MATERIALS, INC.

Chapter 11, Lesson 4, Activity: Using the scrambled letters below, circle every other letter, beginning with the first letter. Use the blank to write the new word created by writing each circled letter in order. (**spatikd**=said) On the title lines, write the title that best describes the words in each column. Choose from these titles: **Places** **People** **Airplanes** **Animals**

Title:

c d h o i r l s d e r b e f n:

t h e u a n c y h u e w r h:

s r i m n p g w e c r g:

Title:

p s a m r a k z:

f n a o r f m e:

l g i h b m r c a d r k y:

Chapter 12, Lesson 2, Activity: Follow the directions below to make "A – An" Fruit Trees. Use these fruits for the activity:

apple **apricot** **cherry** **coconut** **lemon** **orange** **pear** **plum**

Take two large paper bags and draw a giant round (circle) tree with a trunk on each sack. Next, put a large "A" on the top of one tree and a large "An" on the top of the second tree. Then, draw a circle on the appropriate tree for each fruit listed above and write the name of each fruit inside the circle. Color the tree green, the trunk brown, and each circle of fruit a different color.

Finally, go through the house finding five items that begin with a consonant sound to put in the "A" sack and five items that begin with a vowel sound to put in the "An" sack. Then, empty all the items into one big pile. The teacher will time you as you sort each item into the correct bag.

You can do this activity with others in the family. Have other family members put several different items in the sacks and empty the items into a big pile. You can time family and friends as they sort the items into the correct bags.

Chapter 13, Lesson 2, Activity: Find all the prepositions in the boxes below. Then, color each preposition box purple.

to	**cats**	**in**
jets	**on**	**sat**

© SHURLEY INSTRUCTIONAL MATERIALS, INC.

Chapter 14, Lesson 2, Activity: Write the correct prepositions in the blanks. Use these prepositions:

across at by down in on to

Jack was a little brown squirrel that lived _____ a big oak tree. Jack wanted a new adventure. He sat _____ his tree and looked directly _____ the road. That's it! He would go _____ a trip. He would go all the way _____ the road. Then, he would run back _____ his tree.

First, he looked around. The coast was clear. Jack scampered _____ the tree _____ the ground. Next, he ran _____ the yard _____ a big tree _____ the road. He looked around again. Nothing. He took a deep breath and darted _____ the road. There! He had done it! He had gone _____ the road! Wow!

Suddenly, Jack was worried. He heard a sound. Jack was frightened! He ran wildly _____ the road. Then, he dashed back _____ the road. His heart was pounding _____ his chest! He finally got back _____ his tree. He jumped _____ a limb. Then, he climbed rapidly _____ his house. Jack was finally _____ his house. Then, he heard the sound again. Jack took no more chances. He sat contentedly _____ the window and never wanted another adventure.

Chapter 15, Lesson 3, Activity: Use the code in the box below to find transportation words. Using the code numbers, write the correct letters for each blank. Then, make up your own code for several words.

Code		Words										
1. g	10. h											
2. t	11. p	3	10	9	11	15	9	6	16	6	13	5
3. s	12. x											
4. a	13. l	2	4	12	9	2	8	4	6	2	7	8
5. e	14. d											
6. c	15. b											
7. o	16. y	3	13	5	14	2	18	1	15	7	4	2
8. r	17. n											
9. i	18. u	6	4	8	3	2	8	4	9	17	3	

© SHURLEY INSTRUCTIONAL MATERIALS, INC.

Chapter 16, Lesson 3, Activity: In the Word Search Puzzle below, find the following adjective words. The words will appear "down" or "across" in the puzzle. Color the adjectives going down blue and the adjectives going across yellow.

BEAUTIFUL ***BOUNCY*** ***CLEVER*** ***CUTE*** ***EARLY*** ***GIANT***
HUGE ***ORANGE*** ***STRONG*** ***THICK*** ***WEARY*** ***YOUNG***

S	W	E	A	R	L	Y	H	T	C
T	E	A	U	T	I	F	U	H	U
R	A	Y	O	U	N	G	G	I	T
O	R	A	W	O	K	D	E	C	E
N	Y	T	M	P	Q	E	Z	K	B
G	O	S	G	I	A	N	T	U	O
E	C	L	E	V	E	R	O	H	U
H	S	O	R	A	N	G	E	I	N
B	E	A	U	T	I	F	U	L	C
Z	D	U	H	T	E	W	D	K	Y

Chapter 16, Lesson 4, Activity: In the Word Search Puzzle below, find the following preposition words and color each one a different color. The words will appear "down" or "across" in the puzzle.

ACROSS ***AT*** ***BY*** ***DOWN*** ***IN*** ***ON*** ***TO***

A	T	A	B	I	N	E
Y	A	O	N	E	F	D
A	C	R	O	S	S	O
K	O	G	W	H	R	W
B	Y	M	N	T	O	N

Chapter 17, Lesson 4, Activity: In the Word Search Puzzle below, find the following adverb words and color each one a different color. The words will appear "down" or "across" in the puzzle.

HAPPILY ***KINDLY*** ***LOUDLY*** ***RAPIDLY*** ***SILENTLY*** ***SLOWLY*** ***TODAY*** ***WARMLY***

S	K	W	A	R	M	L	Y
I	N	L	J	M	C	E	R
L	K	I	N	D	L	Y	A
E	L	O	U	D	L	Y	P
N	B	D	F	H	S	W	I
T	U	T	O	D	A	Y	D
L	S	L	O	W	L	Y	L
Y	Q	W	E	R	T	U	Y
S	H	A	P	P	I	L	Y

© SHURLEY INSTRUCTIONAL MATERIALS, INC.

Chapter 19, Lesson 3, Activity: Use the code in the box below to find animal words. Using the code numbers, write the correct letters for each blank. Then, make up your own code for several words.

Code		Words										
1. w	10. r											
2. b	11. m	___	___	___	___	___	___	___	___	___	___	
		1	4	7	12	15	17	11	3	7	9	
3. e	12. f											
4. o	13. d											
5. i	14. g	___	___	___	___	___	___	___	___	___	___	___
		14	4	17	8	8	16	10	8	7	3	9
6. n	15. c											
7. l	16. u											
8. t	17. a	___	___	___	___	___	___	___	___	___	___	___
		2	5	10	13	15	18	5	15	19	3	6
9. s	18. h											
	19. k											

Chapter 20, Lesson 5, Activity: In the Word Search Puzzle below, find the following vocabulary words and color each word a color of your choice. All the words begin with the letter *P*. The words will appear "down" or "across."

PARADE PARK PASSENGER PATH PIG PINK PLAYED PONY POOL
POOR POPCORN PORCH PRETTY PROUDLY PUMPKINS PUPPIES PURPLE

P	U	R	P	L	E	P	I	N	K
P	P	X	P	L	P	P	O	N	Y
A	A	P	R	U	O	P	O	O	L
R	S	U	E	M	R	X	P	Z	X
K	S	M	T	Q	C	S	R	P	P
P	E	P	T	A	H	Z	O	A	O
L	N	K	Y	P	I	G	U	R	P
A	G	I	X	C	X	A	D	A	C
Y	E	N	P	A	T	H	L	D	O
E	R	S	P	O	O	R	Y	E	R
D	P	U	P	P	I	E	S	C	N

© SHURLEY INSTRUCTIONAL MATERIALS, INC.

Chapter 23, Lesson 5, Activity: Using the scrambled letters below, circle every other letter, beginning with the first letter. Use the blank to write the new word created by writing each circled letter in order. (**w**pic**n**k**d**=wind) On the title lines, write the title that best describes the words in each column. Choose from these titles: **Science** **Clothes** **Animals** **Verbs**
Title:
r o a y i u n x c t o r a h t:
j h a u c n k y e u t w:
s r o m c p k w s c:
Title:
w s a m l a k b e r d:
s n h o o f u e t w:
s g m h i m l c e d d:

Chapter 26, Lesson 4, Activity: Using the scrambled letters below, circle every other letter, beginning with the first letter. Use the blank to write the new word created by writing each circled letter in order. (**n**pic**n**k**e**=nine) On the title lines, write the title that best describes the words in each column. Choose from these titles: **Colors** **Weather** **Shapes** **Animals**
Title:
t m r y i u a x n o g r l h e:
r n e u c g t y a d n w g p l c e h:
s a q m u p a w r c e w:
Title:
w s i m n a d b y r:
c n l k o a u e d w y:
s g u h n m n c y d:

© SHURLEY INSTRUCTIONAL MATERIALS, INC.